The Very Short Introductions

BLOG BOOK

Original essays written for the OUPblog
from Oxford University Press by authors from
the Very Short Introductions series

Great Clarendon Street, Oxford, OX2 6DP,
United Kingdom

Oxford University Press is a department of the University of Oxford.
It furthers the University's objective of excellence in research, scholarship,
and education by publishing worldwide. Oxford is a registered trade mark of
Oxford University Press in the UK and in certain other countries

British Library Cataloguing in Publication Data

Data available

Library of Congress Cataloging in Publication Data

Data available

ISBN 978–0–19–873243–3

Printed by Bell & Bain Ltd, Glasgow

JOIN OUR COMMUNITY

www.oup.com/vsi

- Join us online at the official Very Short Introductions **Facebook** page.

- Access the thoughts and musings of our authors with our online **blog**.

- Sign up for our monthly **e-newsletter** to receive information on all new titles publishing that month.

- Browse the full range of Very Short Introductions online.

- Read **extracts** from the Introductions for free.

- Visit our library of **Reading Guides**. These guides, written by our expert authors will help you to question again, why you think what you think.

- If you are a teacher or lecturer you can order **inspection copies** quickly and simply via our website.

 Visit the Very Short Introductions website to access all this and more for free:

www.oup.com/vsi

The VERY SHORT INTRODUCTIONS series from Oxford University Press contains hundreds of titles in almost every subject area. These pocket-sized books are the perfect way to get ahead in a new subject quickly. Our expert authors combine facts, analysis, perspective, new ideas, and enthusiasm to make interesting and challenging topics highly readable.

 Praise for the series

"I love the Very Short Introduction Series as should everyone who is interested in the history of ideas. They manage to straddle that difficult line between making the complex accessible without ever compromising on quality. The sheer range of subjects covered make the series an invaluable asset for anyone trying to understand the development of human thought. They are a must-go-to gateway for those of us keen to know more but needing a steer as to where to start."

Claire Fox, Director, Institute of Ideas

"Expert, concise but far from bland, Oxford's 'Very Short Introductions' series must rank by now as a thinking reader's Wikipedia"

Boyd Tonkin, The Independent

Welcome to the VSI Blog Book

Very Short Introductions are the perfect way to get to grips with a new subject quickly. They are trusted by over 7 million people worldwide, and the series now covers over 400 topics.

Our authors are leading experts in their fields, and are as passionate about their subject as they are knowledgeable. Many of them also write for our VSI blog; these articles provide a deeper insight into their particular area and deal with the big questions surrounding their subjects today.

Here we've gathered 30 of their very best blogs. We hope you enjoy this glimpse into the enthusiasm, insight and great writing that characterizes these authors and the *Very Short Introductions* series.

New blogs appear every month on **http://oxford.ly/vsiblog**

Contents

Law

Philosophy

Politics

Religion

Science

Social Science

Arts and Culture

Challenges of the social life of language

By John Edwards

When we consider two obvious facts—that virtually everyone becomes a fluent speaker of at least one language, and that language is central to social life—we can see that most of us are quite sociolinguistically talented. Whether we're consciously aware of it or not, we know quite a lot about many of the intricacies of 'the social life of language'. This doesn't mean, however, that our knowledge is complete or wholly accurate. Here are ten illustrations of the point.

1. Languages and dialects are not the same thing: the former are generally considered as mutually unintelligible—if you speak English, you won't as a consequence expect to understand German—while the latter, as varieties within a language, should be mutually comprehensible. So, if you are a native English speaker from Boston, Massachusetts, you will have little or no trouble understanding someone from Boston, Ontario. Perhaps, however, some difficulty will arise when you speak with yet another Bostonian—from Lincolnshire. Mutual intelligibility can falter, then, as distance increases, and dialects begin to look more like languages. Where to draw the line often becomes a moot point.

2. There are no 'incorrect' or 'illogical' dialects. Every dialectal variety of a language is a rule-governed system adequate for the requirements of its speakers. Grammars may vary across dialects, but the differences are simply that: differences. And, while many of us find some dialects (and languages, for that matter) more pleasant

11

to the ear than others, studies have revealed that no variety is intrinsically more mellifluous. Judgements, whether of grammatical accuracy or of phonetic attractiveness, are largely dependent upon our perceptions of the social standing of the speakers.

3. Everyone is (at least) bilingual. I say this by way of emphasizing that there are no easy measures by which to differentiate bilingual (or multilingual) speakers from their monolingual counterparts. Someone who seems as fluent and comfortable in French as in English certainly appears more bilingual than someone who only knows a few stock phrases ('je ne sais quoi', perhaps, or 'savoir-faire'). But just how much competence should we require before bestowing the 'bilingual' accolade? The difficulty increases when we consider that someone might (for example) be a fluent reader in a second language without being a fluent speaker, or that someone may understand virtually everything but speak only haltingly.

4. (A related point). It is possible to be a very fluent speaker and/or reader of a second (or subsequent) language and yet remain ignorant of subtleties available to native speakers. Interestingly enough, the difficulties here arise at what we might think of as opposite ends of the linguistic spectrum. On the one hand, there is the language of the streets—slang, profanity, idiom, and colloquialism—as well as ironic or comedic usage; on the other, the often dense, allusive, and emotionally nuanced language of poetry. You have to be very well immersed in a language to fully interpret usage at either end of the scale. And this illustrates a more general point: aside from the most mundane of instances, every successful act of communication—even within the same language—involves interpretation.

5. Most languages are related to others, in linguistic 'families'. Many have heard of the Indo-European family, know that both English and German belong to it, and may also be aware that this same grouping includes the Romance varieties (French, Spanish, Portuguese, and so on). Fewer, however, realize that some languages are orphans—

or 'isolates'—and cannot be related to others. Basque, spoken in the Pyrenees between France and Spain, is a contemporary example. It is not an Indo-European variety. Furthermore, its speakers are genetically a little different from other people in that region. The combination of linguistic and genetic variation has of course raised interesting questions about the provenance of the Basque people.

6. Since some language varieties are obviously less prestigious than others, and since their speakers risk becoming the recipients of negative or unfavourable perceptions—reactions that can of course have important social consequences—we might ask why such varieties persist. One reason is that speakers of low social status may be 'marked' by characteristics other than language alone. They might, for instance, look physically different from others. Another, however, is that all dialects reflect and reinforce group identity. My way of speaking may not be socially esteemed, but it remains the language of my family and my community; like all varieties, then, it is a vehicle of culture and social solidarity. You don't sever such a tie lightly.

7. English is the current lingua franca for much of the world and many would argue that it will remain the most important linguistic currency for some time to come. Nonetheless, there is nothing about the language itself that has elevated it to its present position of power: it is in no intrinsic way a 'better' medium than any other. A moment's thought is sufficient to recall the earlier contenders for world language dominance: Greek, Latin, and so on. English is the leading language of our time because of the power possessed by its speakers—that's all. To put it another way: as with other sorts of avenues, all linguistic roads have always led to Rome.

8. Linguistic prescriptivism and purism arise from the belief that corrections, improvements, or protections are needed to safeguard languages. The work of national language academies was historically central here. Once Latin waned as the European lingua franca and local languages emerged into prominence, it became necessary to make choices among dialect variants, to standardize,

to 'fix' languages for purposes of printing. Even then, however, there was the sense that linguistic 'standards' tend to emanate upwards, as it were, from the usage of ordinary speakers. Today most linguistic scholars feel it inappropriate to try and counter this: prescriptivist impulses are now most commonly found among 'ordinary' speakers and others who have strong views about questions of language 'decay', about the terrible language of the younger generation, about the rising tide of slang and profanity, and so on. Yet every maker of a dictionary must be a prescriptivist, and every act of 'language planning'—modernizing a language, for example, or creating an orthography, or intervening on behalf of a 'small' or endangered language—is also necessarily prescriptive. The tensions here are more or less permanent.

9. Language is our prime means of communication, but it is also an important symbol of 'groupness', a marker of belonging, and a vehicle of history, culture, and tradition. The powerful linkage between language and nationalism is the obvious case in point, and there are many examples of people willing to go to the barricades to protect the linguistic symbol of their identity. If language were only a means of communication, we would still expect people to be upset when language shift is forced upon them by social circumstance, but it would not be so easy to understand the intense linguistic zeal of the Québécois, of Celtic revivalists, or of speakers of beleaguered aboriginal languages.

10. Translators have often been looked upon with suspicion, and the point just made, about the linkage between language and group solidarity, is the explanation. Translators are necessary links between communities, but the very ability to straddle linguistic borders may provide access to information that is of mythic, secret, or religious importance. How can we be sure that they are telling others those things—and only those things—that we ask them to? What, after all, are their own cultural allegiances?

■ John Edwards is the author of *Sociolinguistics: A Very Short Introduction*. 978-0-19-985861-3

Book groups and the latest 'it' novel

By Robert Eaglestone

I've never been to a book group (although I was once invited to a dad's 'Listening to the Album of the Month with Beer' club), but I've always been afraid that it would be a bit of a busman's holiday for me, or worse, that—because I'm basically a teacher—it would turn me into the sort of terribly bossy know-it-all you don't want drinking your nicely chilled wine. That said, I often get asked to recommend the current 'it' novel for book groups.

But one of the problems with contemporary fiction is that there is so much written and published all the time that any book, however good, just seems like a drop in the ocean. There is no one 'it' book. So, instead, I'm going to sketch a pattern of what's going on in contemporary fiction to provide a context for reading or choosing a book.

The first thing that's going on at the moment in fiction is a sort of literary playfulness. The '60s and '70s were a heyday of 'experimental fiction' (B. S. Johnson wrote a novel on cards, so that you could shuffle it and read it in any order you chose) and many novels in the '80s and '90s were 'postmodern', playing games with sense, narration, and the very idea of fiction itself. Lots of literary fiction today has, on the one hand, inherited and reused these traditions, but on the other, retreated from their (sometimes quite challenging) extremes. Once thought of as terribly inaccessible, these demanding literary techniques have been domesticated and used in the service of plot and narrative. For example, the British novelist David Mitchell's novel *Cloud Atlas* is made up of interlocking stories, one within the other. One of its main sources of inspiration is the 'classic of postmodernism' *If on a Winter's Night a Traveller* by the Italian writer Italo Calvino. But in Calvino's novel, different stories follow each other and, frustratingly, none of the stories are finished; there is no end. In contrast, in Mitchell's novel, the stories, while interrupted in turn, are finished, making it both more satisfying, but perhaps less memorable.

Linked to this is a return not to the weird experimentalism of the '60s but to older traditions of modernism, to writers like Virginia Woolf and James Joyce, where the form of the novel itself is a central part of its meaning. Ali Smith's brilliant novel, *The Accidental* (2005), is of this sort. The narrative proceeds through the very different consciousnesses of the characters, shifting and playing games with the chronology. The styles change too: one part is written in questions and answers, another uses different styles of love poetry. But the playing with the text tells you as much about what is going on as do the characters.

In contrast to this playfulness in fiction and, equally important, is what can be seen as a turn away from fiction to something more 'real'. The American novelist and critic David Shields has described this as Reality Hunger and discusses writers and artists who are 'breaking larger and larger chunks of "reality" into their works'. This is also happening in other art forms: 'reality TV', verbatim theatre (in which the script is taken from government enquiries, court cases, and so on) and in fine art (where Tracey Emin, for example, takes her experiences as the artwork itself). In writing, one symptom of this is 'popular history'. Kate Summerscale's *The Suspicions of Mr Whicher* reads more like a thriller than a history book, for example. And of course, after Hilary Mantel, there is a huge boom in good historical fiction, which—like your best history teacher—entertains but also seems to tell you about, say, the Tudors. But part of it also comes from writers like W. G. Sebald and Dave Eggers. Sebald's best work, *The Rings of Saturn*, describes a walking tour around Suffolk, and it's unclear whether or not this is fact or fiction. Certainly, it's full of bits of history, all of which circle around the (rather melancholy) themes of destruction and decay. In contrast to this European melancholy is the exuberance of the American writer Dave Eggers. His fiction mixes the real (his first book even included his friends' phone numbers) with the 'shaped', and is packed with jokes and reflections. His later work has become more consciously political: *What Is the What: The Autobiography of Valentino Achak Deng* is by both Eggers (it's called a novel) and a Sudanese 'lost boy' Valentino Achak Deng. It highlights and explains the terrible events in Sudan while making pointed comments about the USA; it's still pretty exuberant though.

Contemporary literary fiction, then, is made up by these two divergent trends—the more experimental, the more seemingly 'real'. They can be picked up in all sorts of fiction (even genre fiction: real-life thrillers, for example) and even in non fiction (who'd have thought that an account of financial mismanagement would be so gripping—but John Lanchester's novelistic account of the credit crunch, *Whoops!*, really is). Perhaps these trends, and their blurring, is telling us something important about the world in which we live.

■ Robert Eaglestone is the author of *Contemporary Fiction: A Very Short Introduction*. 978-0-19-960926-0

Romanticism: a legacy

By Michael Ferber

The *Very Short Introductions* are indeed very short, so I had to cut a chapter out of my volume that would have discussed the aftermath or legacy of Romanticism today, 200 years after Romanticism's days of glory. In that chapter, I would have pointed out the obvious fact that those who still love poetry look at the Romantic era as poetry's high point in every European country. Think of Wordsworth, Keats, Shelley, Pushkin, Mickiewicz, Leopardi, Lamartine, Hugo, and Nerval. Those who still love 'classical' music fill the concert halls to listen to Beethoven, Schumann, Chopin, Berlioz, and Wagner; and those who still love traditional painting flock to look at Constable, Turner, Friedrich, and Delacroix. These poets and artists are still 'alive': their works are central to the culture from which millions of people still draw nourishment. I can scarcely imagine how miserable I would feel if I knew I could never again listen to Beethoven or read a poem by Keats.

But more interesting, I think, is the afterlife of the Romantics in more popular culture. Take William Blake, for instance. Almost a century after he died, Charles Parry set Blake's 16-line poem 'And did those feet in ancient time / Walk upon England's mountains green' to a memorable hymn tune. It was first intended for a patriotic rally during the First World War, but it was soon taken up by the women's suffrage movement and the labour movement because of its moving evocation of a once and future Jerusalem in 'England's green and pleasant land'. It is now England's second national anthem, and is sung in America too: a Connecticut friend of mine always sings 'in New England's green and pleasant land'. It also inspired the title and the music of the 1981 movie *Chariots of Fire*. Emerson, Lake, and Palmer have recorded an acid-rock version of the hymn in 'Brain Salad Surgery' (1973) and Billy Bragg made a more restrained but eloquent one in 1990. In 1948 William Blake 'appeared' to Allen Ginsberg in a hallucination, and thus takes much of the credit (or blame) for the Beat poet's immense poetic works. I often see Blake's 'Proverbs of Hell' as graffiti on walls or as slogans on bumper stickers. When I was an underpaid teaching assistant I joined a picket line carrying a sign I had made: 'The tygers of wrath are wiser than the horses of instruction.' Even as a well-broken-in horse of instruction today I still see much truth in that proverb.

A major legacy of Romanticism is the environmental movement. John Muir (1838–1914), the great pioneer of the wilderness preservation movement, and founder of the Sierra Club, combined a Romantic sensibility with an outlook based on the Bible. He absorbed Burns from his native Scotland, Wordsworth, Coleridge, and Shelley from England, and Emerson and Thoreau from his adopted America. Thoreau himself, who was close to the Transcendentalist group, which grew in large part out of

German and British Romanticism, was the first great nature writer in America; his *Walden* is still required reading not only in universities but among those who are devoted to conservation and sustainability. Wordsworth himself, of course, deserves some credit for his role in preserving the Lake District; he is sometimes called the grandfather of the National Trust of the UK.

It is true that the environmental movement owes much to modern science, and most modern scientists no longer consider Romanticism a useful source of concepts. However, it is also true that without something of the Romantic sensibility, especially the feeling of connectedness to nature or rootedness in the Earth, it would not be much of a movement. 'Organic' metaphors were common among the Romantics, notably the idea that nature is not a mechanism but a living organism and that in an open and imaginative state of mind we can, as Wordsworth put it, 'see into the life of things'. It seems to me that the holistic and ecological outlook owes much to this spirit. Aldo Leopold (1887–1948), famous for his best-selling *Sand County Almanac* with its 'land ethic', writes of the 'biotic community' and the importance of 'thinking like a mountain' to understand the complex interrelationships of humans and nature. And what could be more holistic than the 'Gaia' theory of James Lovelock (born in 1919), according to which the whole Earth acts like one huge organism or ecological unit?

'Romantic' is often a pejorative term, used to dismiss unrealistic, escapist, woolly, or dreamy ideas. But it now seems likely that if we don't soon become a little more Romantic, the Earth will dismiss us.

■ Michael Ferber is the author of *Romanticism: A Very Short Introduction*. 978-0-19-956891-8

Is Renaissance art 'history'?

By Geraldine Johnson

When the latest news in the art world is all about record-breaking prices for contemporary works and the celebrity buzz of events like London's annual Frieze Art Fair, thinking about Renaissance art might seem, well, a little old-fashioned, if not downright eccentric. But if the two experiences I had recently are anything to go by, maybe we need to think again.

The first of these occurred during an art history class I was teaching to a group of newly arrived Master's students, fizzing with intellectual energy and excitement. The topic was how the concept of 'the artist' had changed in European culture from ancient times to the present day, with an intriguing sideways glance at the situation in pre-modern China. By the end of the usual give-and-take of a graduate seminar, it had become clear to all of us that there were actually a surprising number of similarities between that first great celebrity artist, the 'divine' Michelangelo, and much more recent art-world superstars.

As we know all too well from countless biographies, exhibitions, films, and television specials, 19th and early 20th century rebel-artists seemed to gain critical acclaim in the long run (indeed, often only after they had died) by very overtly rejecting all trappings of worldly success. Think of Gauguin giving up a career as a big-city stockbroker to live in faraway Tahiti; or van Gogh being unable to sell almost any paintings during his own lifetime. In contrast, Michelangelo, Dürer, Titian, Bernini, Rubens, and many other Renaissance and Baroque artists were absolutely desperate to become rich, famous, and if at all possible ennobled, and were clearly thrilled at the prospect of hanging out with popes and princes. This, in many ways, seems much closer to the red-carpet appearances, VIP-fraternizing, and multi-millionaire tastes of Damien Hirst, Tracey Emin, and Grayson Perry than to those old garret-loving, poverty-stricken members of the Modernist avant-garde. The lifestyle choices and self-conscious PR strategies of contemporary celebrity artists may thus have more in common with Michelangelo than with Manet or Matisse than one might at first think.

Another event that convinced me that Renaissance art is far from 'history' was the phone conversation I had immediately after my class had finished. A reporter from the *Wall Street Journal* had called to ask me to provide some background information for an article she was writing on changing reactions to nude men versus nude women in art. The catalyst was the opening of a new exhibition in Vienna's Leopold Museum entitled 'Nackte Männer' or 'Nude Men', which rather predictably was generating a great deal of controversy even before the first ticket had been sold.

Once again, contemporary art practices could only be fully understood by looking back in time. Initially, one had to turn to the art academies of the 17th, 18th, and 19th centuries that privileged using the nude male model in art education and thus, by definition, made it nearly impossible for respectable young women to be trained in anything other than painting demure still lives and fully clothed portraits. But ultimately, to find the sources for the almost endless academic studies of nude men—not to mention the four-metre-high photographic installation known as 'Mr Big' that was parked in front of the Leopold Museum—one had to go back to the future once again in the form of Renaissance artists such as Michelangelo, who saw the male rather than the female body as the ideal human form, and who themselves looked even further back to the Classical bodies of ancient Roman and Greek sculpture.

During the run of the 'Nackte Männer' exhibition in Vienna, large red stickers were hastily pasted onto the exposed genitals of the three naked male athletes whose photograph by French artists Pierre & Gilles was used on the exhibition posters plastered throughout the city, much to the distress of the more delicate members of the Austrian public. Back in Michelangelo's day, it was painted loincloths that were retroactively added to cover the bare buttocks (and worse) of the saints and sinners depicted in his 'Last Judgment' in the Sistine Chapel, with the censorship carried out, in this case, at the behest of incensed clerics, convinced that the pope's chapel was being turned into a brothel. So, what goes around, really does come around, if you know your Renaissance art. And, funnily enough, there were even some 'old masters' on display at a spin-off of the most recent Frieze Art Fair in London.

■ Geraldine Johnson is the author of *Renaissance Art: A Very Short Introduction*. 978-0-19-280354-2

Arts & Culture

Colonial Latin American Literature
Rolena Adorno
9780199755028

Comedy
Matthew Bevis
9780199601714

Contemporary Art
Julian Stallabrass
9780192806468

Contemporary Fiction
Robert Eaglestone
9780199609260

Dada and Surrealism
David Hopkins
9780192802545

Design
John Heskett
9780192854469

Dictionaries
Lynda Mugglestone
9780199573790

Documentary Film
Patricia Aufderheide
9780195182705

Early Music
Thomas Forrest Kelly
9780199730766

Egyptian Myth
Geraldine Pinch
9780192803467

English Literature
Jonathan Bate
9780199569267

Ethnomusicology
Timothy Rice
9780199794379

The Etruscans
Christopher Smith
9780199547913

Film
Michael Wood
9780192803535

Film Music
Kathryn Kalinak
9780195370874

Folk Music
Mark Slobin
9780195395020

French Literature
John D. Lyons
9780199568727

German Literature
Nicholas Boyle
9780199206599

The Gothic
Nick Groom
9780199586790

Hieroglyphs
Penelope Wilson
9780192805027

Humour
Noël Carroll
9780199552221

Italian Literature
David Robey & Peter Hainsworth
9780199231799

Journalism
Ian Hargreaves
9780199686872

Kafka
Ritchie Robertson
9780192804556

Languages
Stephen Anderson
9780199590599

Landscape Architecture
Ian Thompson
9780199681204

Late Antiquity
Gillian Clark
9780199546206

Linguistics
P. H. Matthews
9780192801487

Literary Theory
Jonathan Culler
9780199691340

The Marquis de Sade
John Phillips
9780192804693

Modern Latin American Literature
Roberto Gonzalez Echevarria
9780199754915

Modern Art
David Cottington
9780192803641

Modernism
Christopher Butler
9780192804419

Music
Nicholas Cook
9780192853820

The New Testament as Literature
Kyle Keefer
9780195300208

The Orchestra
D. Kern Holoman
9780199760282

Photography
Steve Edwards
9780192801647

Postmodernism
Christopher Butler
9780192802392

Poststructuralism
Catherine Belsey
9780192801807

Prehistory
Chris Gosden
9780192803436

Renaissance Art
Geraldine A. Johnson
9780192803542

Rhetoric
Richard Toye
9780199651368

Roman Britain
Peter Salway
9780192854049

Romanticism
Michael Ferber
9780199568918

Russian Literature
Catriona Kelly
9780192801449

Science Fiction
David Seed
9780199557455

Shakespeare
Germaine Greer
9780192802491

Sociolinguistics
John Edwards
9780199858613

Spanish Literature
Jo Labanyi
9780199208050

Theatre
Marvin Carlson
9780199669820

Tragedy
Adrian Poole
9780192802354

Writing and Script
Andrew Robinson
9780199567782

Business and Economics

Innovating with technology

By Mark Dodgson and David Gann

The next big thing in innovation lies in the ways we innovate using technology. We're used to thinking about innovations that are technologies—the computer, the Internet, the laser, and so on. But technology is now being used to produce better innovations than ever before. By better, we mean innovations that meet our personal, organizational, and social requirements in new and improved ways, and aren't just reliant on the technical skills and imagination of corporate engineers and marketers.

Here are some examples of what we mean. If you have ever been lucky enough to design and build a home, you would have been confronted by technical drawings that are incomprehensible to anyone but trained architects. Nowadays you can have a computerized model of your house that lets you move around it in virtual reality so that you get a high-fidelity sense of the layout and feel of rooms. You get to know what it really will look like, and make changes to it, before a brick is laid.

Move up a level and consider the challenges confronting the redesign of Cannon Street Station in London. This project involved not only redesigning the station, but also building an office block above it, whilst maintaining access to the fully operational Underground station beneath it. The project used augmented reality technology to assist the design and planning process. Using a smartphone or tablet, augmented reality overlays a digital model on the surrounding real world, so you can see hidden infrastructure such as optical fibres, sewers, and gas lines—and get a sense of what things will look like before work begins. This is especially valuable for dealing with various vintages of infrastructure in busy city environments and when there are concerns about maintaining the integrity of listed buildings. The key principle in these examples is that non-specialists can become involved in decisions that were previously only made by experts.

Other technologies that encourage this 'democratization' of innovation include rapid prototyping. This technology changes the economics of manufacturing, so it becomes feasible to make bespoke, individualized products cheaply. If you design something yourself, you don't need expensive moulds, dies, and machine tools to make it. We are quickly developing technologies that can produce your designs on the spot on your desk.

The Internet underlies much of the advance in the ways we innovate. It allows us to collect information from a massively increased population of designers, producers, and users of innovation. It connects ideas, people, and organizations. Also important is the 'Internet of things'—that is the vast number of mobile devices and sensors that are connected together and produce data that can be valuably used to make better decisions. Drivers' mobile phones, for example, can locate cars and traffic jams and allow better planning of transport flows. We have it from a reputable source that more transistors—the building blocks of sensors and mobile devices—were produced last year than grains of rice were grown. And they were produced at a lower unit cost.

We're all much better attuned at processing images rather than text and data. Half our cerebral cortex is devoted to visualization. Technologies developed in the computer games and film industries—think *Toy Story* and *World of Warcraft*—are being used to help innovators in areas ranging from pharmaceuticals to emergency response units in cities. The capacity which these new technologies bring to produce dynamic images of what was previously opaque technical information underlies the greater engagement in innovation by a wider range of people.

The technology that seems likely to have the greatest impact globally on innovation is the smartphone. Just think how short a period of time we've been using them and yet how much we use them for. Quite apart from putting us in direct contact with the majority in the world's population, we use them to shop, bank, pay bills, and map our way. We use a myriad apps for all sorts of productive and entertaining purposes. Nearly six billion of the world's seven billion people have mobile phones and in many developing countries there are more mobiles than people.

These devices provide opportunities for innovation amongst billions of people that have previously been excluded from the global economy for lack of information and money. Smartphones provide everyone with access to all the staggering amount of information available on the web. They can also allow access to finance, especially small amounts of money. Less than two billion people in the world have bank accounts, and banking on smartphones allows billions of previously disenfranchised people to borrow, trade, and be reimbursed for their ideas and initiative. In this way, technology makes innovation more inclusive and less the privilege of corporations with research and development departments. We look forward to a massive wave of exciting new and unimaginable ideas from all sorts of people from everywhere around the world.

■ Mark Dodgson and David Gann are the authors of *Innovation: A Very Short Introduction*. 978-0-19-956890-1

Permission-giving: from Cromwell to Kate Middleton

By Keith Grint

Some of my more radical academic colleagues remain inordinately sceptical of the role of individual leaders set against the tectonic plates of economic systems, social classes, genders, political alliances, and ethnic groups. To suggest that individual leaders might make a difference is to place an unwarranted responsibility upon mere actors when the real issue is 'the system'—whatever the system is. However, I want to suggest that we look again at permission-giving as just one aspect that encourages or discourages followers from specific acts. Let me turn to an apocryphal story from the Korean War to illustrate this. As in the Second World War, the American Army (like the British army, but unlike the German army) removed discretion at the lower echelons and deposited most knowledge and decision-making within the officer corps. As a consequence when Allied troops landed on D-Day in Normandy, German soldiers targeted Allied officers as the most effective way to immobilize the invaders. In the Korean War little seemed to have changed; when American soldiers were captured, their North Korean captors frequently resorted to torturing American officers—since the ordinary soldiers seldom had significant information—and as a consequence American soldiers were required to strip their emblems of rank if capture looked likely. This left the North Koreans with a problem: how to determine the officers amongst a group of captured US soldiers? The result, according to the apocryphal version of events, was that one enterprising North Korean interrogator demanded that all the American soldiers in his charge remove their trousers—at which point everyone looked at their officer for permission to strip.

This 'permission-giving' aspect of leadership is a critical, and critically underrated, aspect. In Neil Mitchell's book, *Agents of Atrocity*, he argues that leaders make a crucial difference in the occurrence, or prevention, of human rights abuses through their permission-giving. Thus rather than assuming that context determines the actions of leaders he suggests that leaders always retain a degree of choice in both their, and their followers', actions. In effect, some leaders allow or even encourage their followers to engage in mass rape and murder after conquest, while others actively prevent it. The most interesting case is Oliver Cromwell. In the English aspect of the English Civil War the pillaging of captured cities was common on both sides until the rise of the

Parliamentary New Model Army under Cromwell. That group was specifically forbidden from engaging in the rape, murder, and looting that hitherto had been commonplace. In contrast, when Cromwell led the army into Ireland he didn't actively prevent any such brutality, and the consequences were the sacking and butchery of Drogheda and Wexford.

Note here that the critical point is how leaders and their followers are not driven into bestial behaviour as a response to a bestial situation; on the contrary, and in sharp contrast to contingency theory, what people do is a consequence of the choices they make, albeit constrained choices. This being the case we might look afresh at whether we should focus on the provision of material sustenance in areas of conflict—water, food, money, jobs, security, and so on—or turn instead to the ideological aspects of life. We know historically that people in terrible material conditions don't automatically revolt when food is short or jobs are scarce. They revolt when an alternative appears viable to a terrible present. We can see this captured in the history of slavery. It was probably common to almost all forms of prior human society and is usually linked to terrible material circumstances, but revolts aren't a permanent or ever present feature of slave history.

When we apply this to other aspects of society it becomes clear just how important leadership is in its permission-giving—or withholding—capacity. Public assaults upon the Jews in Germany were significantly increased once Hitler had publicly denounced Jews. At the same time racist statements in public in the UK are now much rarer than they used to be because the leading role of the law and the political establishment has rendered such comments beyond the pale. But we do not need to wander into the political arena to notice the importance of permission-giving. According to the *Guardian*, the Queen's adoption of the Stocky Heel shoe is responsible for the surge in demand, and we only have to watch whatever Kate Middleton is wearing to see sales of the same dress race out of the shops. Permission-giving even affects suicide patterns with copy-cat suicides being common.

Might it be then, that a hugely important aspect of leadership is not so much what 'the situation' or the 'system' determines or facilitates but what individual leaders permit or prohibit through their active or passive leadership?

■ Keith Grint is the author of *Leadership: A Very Short Introduction*. 978-0-19-956991-5

Management for humans

By John Hendry

The word 'management' derives from the 16th century Italian *maneggiare*—to handle or control a horse. The application has been extended over the centuries from horses to weapons, boats, sports people, and nowadays to people and affairs quite generally, but the connotation of control remains. Indeed, in management theory, as we teach it in business schools, control is a central preoccupation. Theories differ in the assumptions they make about human motivation and behaviour, and in the organizational structures, incentives, reward systems, and managerial techniques they prescribe. Some treat working people as willing or unwilling cogs in a machine, to be disciplined so as to maximize the efficiency of the machine. Others treat them as enterprising but self-interested individuals, to be manipulated through incentives to do what is required. Still others see them as cooperative problem-solvers, to be harnessed to an organization's culture and goals. But all seek to control them in one way or another so as to maximize their output or efficiency. The words discipline, manipulate, and harness could all be applied equally well to that 16th century horse.

In real life, of course, people are not horses, and while most managers would like to be in control they rarely are. Most large organizations employ structures and techniques based on management theories, and use these to exert some kind of control. Many small organizations still operate by more traditional methods of control: 'do as you're told or else'. But for most managers, in whatever kind of organization, management is as much about coping, and helping others to cope, as it is about controlling: 'How are you doing? I'm managing.'

We wouldn't give somebody the job title of 'coper'. It doesn't sound nearly authoritative enough. But we don't generally give them the title of 'controller' either. We know that managers often aren't in control, and to describe them as controllers would only invite sarcasm. (Sir Topham Hatt, the benign 'fat controller' of the *Thomas the Tank Engine* stories, acquired his job title on the nationalization of the railways in 1948, when obesity was not considered a problem and war-time notions of what could be achieved by centralized planning and direction still prevailed)! But as any parent will tell you, coping is very important. The central challenge for managers, as for parents, is less about controlling and more about coping when, through no fault of one's own, things begin to get out of control.

Whatever kind of business or service you are engaged in, the most challenging aspect of management is trouble-shooting, or responding to what the British Prime Minister Harold Macmillan famously termed 'events'. Unplanned, unexpected, and often unwanted events happen. Things go wrong. Machines break down. Supplies get delayed. Workers strike. Competitors steal a march. Customers get upset, with or without good reason. Projects go over budget. Deadlines get missed. Tasks get forgotten, or fall through the cracks. People get ill or have accidents at critical moments. People make mistakes. People get convinced that other people have made mistakes. Colleagues fall out. Rumours spread. The best laid plans go awry and things don't work out as intended.

This is life. It has to be dealt with, and the only way it can be dealt with is through the very human process of talking to people and working things out. Situations need to be explained and understood. Conflicts need to be resolved and tensions eased. Mistakes, including the manager's own mistakes, need to be recognized and rectified. People need to be admonished or forgiven, and helped to do better.

Theories of management control are of little help here. You have to work with individual human beings and their actual motivations and behaviours, not with what theories might assume. You have to work, too, with their individual conceptions of the world and how it works, and with their individual concerns and preoccupations, their likes and dislikes, their moods and emotions. The management literature can still offer valuable insights, however.

The literature on sense-making, for example, helps us to understand how people make sense of the world and how the sense they make of it adapts to new circumstances. One of the very important things that managers do is make sense of things for the employees reporting to them, explaining what the organization is about and how their work fits into it, for example. And one of the challenges when things go wrong is to make sense of what has happened and why, giving them a story that fits both with the grander organizational story and with their own personal life stories, on the basis of which they can adapt and move on.

The ethics of management are also important here. Though 'business ethics' is sometimes dismissed as an oxymoron, the fact is that managers are human beings, the people they manage are human beings, and, no matter what the setting, the relationships between any human beings are moral relationships. A good manager, like a good friend, will be compassionate and caring, truthful and fair, human-hearted, to use an Eastern term, or loving, to use a Western one. Of course, we would never put the word 'loving' in a manager's job description, just as we would never put in the word 'coping'. It's not scientific enough, not sufficiently output-oriented; it smacks of inefficiency and softness when we want to signal efficiency and hard results. But I don't think you can manage well without it.

■ John Hendry is the author of *Management: A Very Short Introduction*. 978-0-19-965698-1

Business and Economics

Accounting
Christopher Nobes
9780199684311

Advertising
Winston Fletcher
9780199568925

Capitalism
James Fulcher
9780192802187

Choice Theory
Michael Allingham
9780192803030

**Corporate Social
Responsibility**
Jeremy Moon
9780199671816

Economics
Partha Dasgupta
9780192853455

Entrepreneurship
Paul Westhead
& Mike Wright
9780199670543

Environmental Economics
Stephen Smith
9780199583584

Game Theory
Ken Binmore
9780199218462

Global Economic History
Robert C. Allen
9780199596652

**The Great Depression and
New Deal**
Eric Rauchway
9780195326345

Innovation
Mark Dodgson
& David Gann
9780199568901

Keynes
Robert Skidelsky
9780199591640

Leadership
Keith Grint
9780199569915

Malthus
Donald Winch
9780199670413

Management
John Hendry
9780199656981

Microeconomics
Avinash Dixit
9780199689378

Organizations
Mary Jo Hatch
9780199584536

Risk
Baruch Fischhoff
& John Kadvany
9780199576203

**The World Trade
Organization**
Amrita Narlikar
9780192806086

Work
Stephen Fineman
9780199699360

History

The Reign of Terror

By William Doyle

Two hundred and twenty-one years ago (on 5 September 1793) saw the official beginning of the Terror in the French Revolution. Ever since that time, it is very largely what the French Revolution has been remembered for. When people think about it, they picture the guillotine in the middle of Paris, surrounded by baying mobs, ruthlessly chopping off the heads of the king, the queen, and innumerable aristocrats for months on end in the name of liberty, equality, and fraternity. It was social and political revenge in action. The gory drama of it has proved an irresistible background to writers of fiction, whether Charles Dickens's *Tale of Two Cities*, or Baroness Orczy's *Scarlet Pimpernel* novels, or many other depictions on stage and screen. It is probably more from these, rather than more sober historians, that the English-speaking idea of the French Revolution is derived.

Unquestionably the Terror was bloody. Over 16,000 people were officially condemned to death, as many again or more probably lost their lives in less official ways, and tens of thousands were imprisoned as suspects, many of them dying in prison rather than under the blade of the guillotine. But the French Revolution did not begin with Terror, and nobody planned it in advance. Robespierre, so often (and quite wrongly) regarded as its architect, was a vocal opponent of capital punishment when the Revolution began. But revolutions, simply because they aim to destroy what went before, create enemies. In France there were probably far more losers than winners, and not all of those who lost were prepared to accept their fate. So from the start there were growing numbers of counter-revolutionaries, dreaming of overturning the new order. How were they to be dealt with?

After three years of increasing polarization, it was decided to force everybody to choose by launching a war. In war nobody can opt out: you are on our side or on theirs, and if you're on theirs, you're a traitor. If the war goes badly, it becomes increasingly tempting to blame it on treason, and to crack down on everybody suspected of it. By the first quarter of 1793, the war was going badly. The first proven traitor to suffer official punishment was the king himself, overthrown in August 1792 and executed the following January. After that the new republic found itself on the defensive against most of Europe. The measures it took to organize the war effort, including conscripting young men for the armies, provoked widespread rebellion throughout the country. By the summer huge stretches of the western countryside were out of control, and major cities of the south were denouncing the tyranny of Paris. When news came in early September that Toulon, the great Mediterranean naval base, had surrendered to the British, the populace of Paris mobbed the ruling Convention and forced it to declare Terror the order of the day. It seemed the only way to defeat the republic's internal enemies.

Many of the instruments of Terror were already in place. A revolutionary tribunal had been established in March, and the guillotine had first been used a year earlier, designed as a reliable, fast, and humane way of executing criminals. Now they were systematically turned against rebels. Most victims of the Terror died in the provinces, after forces loyal to the Convention recaptured centres of resistance. This was mopping up a civil war. The vast majority of them were not aristocrats but ordinary people caught up in conflicts that they could not avoid. Naturally, however, it was high-profile victims who caught the eye, especially when, in the early summer of 1794, political justice was centralized in Paris. Often called the 'great' Terror, these last few months actually represented an attempt to bring the process under control. By then people were so sickened by the bloodshed (for unlike hanging, decapitation did shed a lot of blood) that the main site of execution was moved to the suburbs. The emergency was in fact over, and repression had done its work. The fortunes of war had also turned, and French armies were winning again. So everybody was looking for ways to end an episode of which the republic was becoming increasingly ashamed. Eventually a scapegoat was found, Robespierre, who had too often stood up to defend the increasingly indefensible.

Terror had built up slowly, and the proclamation of 5 September 1793 merely confirmed what was already happening. But it ended quite suddenly in July 1794, when it was possible to pin the blame shared by many on one incautiously vocal figure and a handful of his henchmen. But however ruthlessly, Terror had saved the republic from overthrow. Nor should we forget that other combatant states at the time resorted to repression of their own. In 1798, 30,000 people died in the great Irish rebellion, in a population only a sixth that of France. The British monarchy could be every bit as ruthless as the French republic—when it had to be.

■ William Doyle is the author of *The French Revolution: A Very Short Introduction*. 978-0-19-285396-7

Why are Russians attracted to strong leaders?

By Geoffrey Hosking

After a decade of a chaotic but exhilarating democracy in the 1990s, Vladimir Putin as president and prime minister has been restoring a strong state. At least, that is how we usually understand it. He has certainly restored an authoritarian state. On assuming office in 2000, he strengthened the 'power vertical' by ending the local election of provincial governors and sending in his own viceroys—mostly ex-military men—to supervise them. Citing the state's need for 'information security', he closed down or took over media outlets which exposed inconvenient information or criticized his actions. Determined opponents were bankrupted, threatened, arrested, even murdered. He subdued the unruly Duma (parliament) by making it much more difficult for opposition parties to register or gain access to the media, and by encouraging violations of electoral procedure at the polls. Until recently, the Russian public seemed to accept this as part of the natural order.

This is all part of a well-established historical pattern. There are good reasons for Russians' attachment to strong leaders. They fear both external invasion and internal subversion. A glance at their history reveals why. Their frontiers are very long and open, and over the centuries they have suffered invasion many times. In 1237 the Mongol onslaught brought devastation of towns and mass murder or enslavement of citizens. In Suzdal, for example, according to the *Chronicle*,

> They plundered the Church of the Holy Virgin and burned down the prince's court and burned down the Monastery of St Dmitrii, and the others they plundered. The old monks and nuns and priests and the blind, lame, hunchbacked and sick they killed, and the young monks and nuns and priests and priests' wives and deacons and deacons' wives, and their daughters and sons—all were led away into captivity.

Older people can still remember the German invasion of 1941, in which such scenes were reproduced over broad swathes of the country. Russians will support almost any regime which offers them security from attack, even if they distrust and resent the local officials with whom they have everyday dealings. And that means that almost any regime can legitimize itself by claiming that Russia is in danger. Putin has done so by insinuating that NATO is threatening Russia militarily and subverting it from within through foreign-financed, non-governmental organizations. The latter accusation resonates with Russians, since they also fear troublemaking underlings inside the country. Three times in the last four centuries the Russian state has collapsed: in the early-17th century 'time of troubles', in the revolution of 1917–21, and in the collapse of the USSR in 1991–3. In the first two cases the result was civil war, and that nearly happened in 1993 as well. Even without civil war, if the state is weak, rich and powerful local bosses can throw their weight about unrestrained. They enrich themselves and their clients, seize the property of opponents, and beat them up or murder them, if they see fit. Russians still vividly remember the 1990s, when state property was dispersed among oligarchs, and as a result many hospitals, schools, and old people's homes became impoverished and decrepit, while pensioners, teachers, and nurses were paid late in inflated rubles—if at all.

These memories help to explain why Putin is still trusted by many Russians, especially those of the older generation. Under him material life has greatly improved. But this is largely because the price of Russia's main export, oil, has soared. Trust in Putin is wary and was declining even before autumn 2011. Russians are aware that he encourages or at least tolerates unsavoury practices which damage their lives. They know that their immediate superiors are corrupt and overbearing, and that redress for abuses is unattainable. An authoritarian state is not necessarily a strong state. On the contrary, rather than enforce the law, it may merely co-opt greedy underlings and license their depredations.

Here too Russians are re-enacting familiar scenarios. In past centuries serfs generally accepted their lot as necessary and in any case ineluctable. Besides, it offered them modest benefits: some cultivable land and membership in a village community which usually ran its own affairs by negotiation with the landlord's steward. (The British Empire, by contrast, could not manage without enclosures, the Poor Law, and the workhouse). But there were always discontented serfs who escaped the burdens and injustices to resettle in the Empire's open frontier lands. If opportunity offered, moreover, or if new abuses were inflicted on them, even the peasants who stayed at home could and did cause serious trouble. There were massive rebellions in the 1660s, 1770s, 1905–6, and 1917–18, and continual smaller scale protests in between.

Nowadays there are no more serfs in the literal sense, but ordinary citizens often feel like semi-serfs. Young professional people find their careers blocked by local power brokers; businessmen in official disfavour see their premises raided, their tax affairs minutely examined, and sometimes their businesses bankrupted. Many of them have visited or even lived in other countries; they know that at least in some of these the authorities are restrained by the rule of law. They would like to see it established in Russia too.

That is why, when the parliamentary elections of December 2011 were blatantly falsified, the passivity abruptly ended. Massive protest demonstrations took place in the major cities, calling for a rerun of the elections and 'Russia without Putin'. Young professional and commercial people, using the new social networking sites, were at the core of the demonstrations. But many ordinary workers, pensioners, and others participated too. There was no mistaking the widespread anger and resentment. They all know that the state is not doing its proper job of enforcing the law.

It is impossible to tell at the moment whether the population will once more relapse into sullen acquiescence, or whether an effective opposition movement will take shape. Nor can we tell whether Putin, who was back in full power as president from May 2012, will continue to crush his opponents by force, or whether he will introduce serious reforms. What we do know from the past, however, is that once change starts in Russia it tends to be cumulative and sweeping, and to result in greater changes than seemed possible at the outset. We also know that when Russians yearn for a strong state, they also yearn for a just one.

■ Geoffrey Hosking is the author of *Russian History: A Very Short Introduction*. 978-0-19-958098-9

The legacy of the Napoleonic Wars

By Mike Rapport

The Duke of Wellington always has a traffic cone on his head. At least, he does when he is in Glasgow. Let me explain: outside the city's Gallery of Modern Art on Queen Street, there is an equestrian statue of the celebrated general of the Napoleonic Wars. It was sculpted in 1840–4 by the Franco-Italian artist, Carlo Marochetti (1805–67), who in his day was a dominant figure in the world of commemorative sculpture. Amongst his works is the statue of Richard the Lionheart, who has sat on his mount and held aloft his sword outside the Houses of Parliament since 1860.

Yet Glasgow's lofty monument has been a magnet for pranksters—ever since the 1980s, according to the BBC—who regularly scale the pedestal, Copenhagen's (the horse's) flanks and then, clinging onto the Iron Duke himself, crown him with an orange traffic cone. This has caused some controversy: the police warn that the acts of intrepid, late-night climbers (who, to be frank, may also have enjoyed the hospitality of the local hostelries) is an act of vandalism and is downright dangerous. The government-funded agency that oversees the care of the country's historic buildings, Historic Scotland, acknowledges that embellishing Wellington with a modern piece of traffic paraphernalia is now a 'longstanding tradition', but emphasizes that the statue is A-listed and so needs to be protected from damage—and there has indeed been damage: on different occasions, the general has lost a spur and his sword. Others argue that the 'coning' of Wellington is a worthy expression of the people's sense of humour and that it is as much a part of the cityscape as its historic buildings and monuments. And indeed the statue has become iconic—not because it is a likeness of the Duke of Wellington, but because the general has a cone on his head: postcards proudly depicting this symbol of Glaswegian humour are easy to find.

This controversy sprang to mind when I was first putting together a proposal for writing a *Very Short Introduction* on the Napoleonic Wars. One of the reviewers very helpfully suggested that the book might consider a chapter on the conflict in historical memory and commemoration. When I came to write this, the final chapter, I considered opening it with an account of the 'coning' of the Duke of Wellington, but in the end I felt that such irreverence and jocularity sat rather uneasily with the content of the rest of the book, which tells a tale of aggression, international collapse, and human suffering. Yet the fact that the Duke still sits, as ever, with a garish point on his head—gravity making it lean at a jaunty angle—did make me wonder about how far the Napoleonic Wars (including, by extension, the French Revolutionary Wars from which they emerged—collectively the wars lasted from 1792 to 1815) have left a legacy that is embedded, visibly or otherwise, in our European cityscapes.

This might well be more obvious on the continent than in the British Isles, since there was a direct impact as armies rampaged across Europe—and there were therefore more sites clearly associated with Napoleonic conquest, European resistance to it, and later commemoration of the conflict. In Paris, the very same Marochetti was responsible for one of the reliefs on the Arc de Triomphe in Paris, the one depicting the Battle of Jemappes (one of the French Revolution's early victories over the Austrians in 1792). The Arc was completed under the July Monarchy (1830–48), which worked hard to appropriate the Napoleonic legacy for its own political purposes. The same regime nearly awarded Marochetti the commission to create Napoleon's tomb in the Church of the Invalides when his body was repatriated from Saint Helena. The sculptor, in fact, was producing models for this work as he was busy on Glasgow's Wellington statue (giving the latter a pedigree that surely reinforces Historic Scotland's mild-mannered point). Yet British towns and cities are also embedded with places that are connected with the French Wars—as barracks, headquarters, places of exile and refuge, naval dockyards, depots for prisoners of war, as sites of popular mobilization. Sometimes the associations are long-forgotten, sometimes they are commemorated. The conflict is remembered in the monuments that ask us not to forget the carnage and in the individuals who are commemorated in stone and bronze. These may, like Glasgow's Iron Duke, have become so much part of our urban environment that they are almost unnoticed unless they have a cone on their head, but the traces and memory of the French wars in Britain's towns and cities . . . now there's a project!

■ Mike Rapport is the author of *The Napoleonic Wars: A Very Short Introduction*. 978-0-19-959096-4

Witchcraft: yesterday and today

By Malcolm Gaskill

I'm looking at a photo of my 6-year-old daughter wearing her witch costume—black taffeta and pointy hat—last Halloween. Our local vicar marked the occasion by lamenting in the parish magazine this 'celebration of evil'. All Hallows' Eve, the night when traditionally folk comforted souls of the dead, is not, in fact, evil, but did once have evil in its margins. Spirits on the loose might be bad as well as good, and for humans to manipulate them was considered witchcraft. The perception of evil, concentrated in the figure of the witch, was once powerfully real. Kate's fancy dress character, however winsome, has a profound cultural connection to a terrifying dimension of the past and, as we'll see, the present too.

Myths about the 'witch-craze' abound. One version has it that millions of medieval women were persecuted by the Church, aided by the prejudices of benighted peasants. Witchcraft accusations, we like to think, were a good way for people stupider than us to get rid of people they didn't like or who they chose to scapegoat to explain misfortune in an unscientific age. This picture is essentially false. The 'witch-hunt' resulted in the execution of around 50,000 people (a fifth of them men), mostly in the 16th and 17th centuries. A key development at that time was the rise of the State, with its laws and tribunals, and it was this, far more than the Catholic Church, which made witch-hunting possible. Insofar as religion was involved, it was the ferocious energy unleashed by the Protestant Reformation that did most harm. Finally, if witchcraft was a pretext to bump off enemies, it wasn't a very good one: about half of all suspicions—the few that made it into court—ended in acquittals. In England, three-quarters of all trials disappointed the accusers.

And this was no cultural dark age. These were the days of Shakespeare, Milton, and Newton—no longer the Middle Ages. It was the Early Modern period with its new sciences and tech-nologies, literary and artistic genius, explosions of print and commerce, global discoveries, and new ways of seeing and feeling. It's more comfortable to think that witch-hunts preceded the Renaissance, but they didn't, and if we look closely we can see why. The search for truth, and growing human confidence to find it, underpinned the inquisitorial legal process, replacing blind faith in judicial ordeals and unlimited torture. Statutes against witches and the will to use them, combined with social and economic tension caused by demographic change, largely explain the rise of witch-trials after 1500. Witches were made officially real by law and reason long before the same law and reason made them unreal by undermining the evidence on which they were tried.

What is remarkable is, even in the heyday of witchcraft prosecutions, just how much restraint was shown in most places, at most times. There was no witch-holocaust because communities and authorities alike were preoccupied with order, and con-demning innocent people did not serve that end. England went through a few years, during the Civil Wars, when settled life was disturbed, puritan magistrates and clergy became powerful, and the normal administration of justice was interrupted. Once restraints were removed, what followed was the most savage witch-hunt in English history, with perhaps 300 East Anglian women and men accused, and a third of them executed.

But throughout Europe and colonial North America, such events were the exceptions that proved the rule, the rule being that witch-crazes were uncommon and undesired by most. During our Halloween fun, it's worth remembering both those who died and those who were sufficiently sceptical and fond of communal harmony to keep mass witch-hunts at bay. And we might also remember that the distance between us and such outrages is not just a few hundred years, but a few thousand miles.

On 6 February 2013, Kepari Leniata, a 20-year-old mother of two living in the highlands of Papua New Guinea, was accused of bewitching a 6-year-old boy to death. Villagers stripped and bound her, then dragged her to a rubbish dump where she was tortured with hot irons until she confessed. The police arrived, but were held back by locals who doused Leniata in petrol and burned her alive. The UN human rights office explained that this was just the latest of numerous lynchings, each conforming to a pattern found in many parts of the developing world where witch-beliefs are strong and uncontained by law or authority.

The persecution of witches in any age says a lot about the society that allows it or cannot resist it—its structures, institutions, and social organization of power. If we in the West have successfully neutralized our most deadly fears and packaged our persecutions as harmless trick-or-treating, then perhaps we shouldn't be too worried about whether, in doing so, we are celebrating evil. Recent events in Papua New Guinea suggest that we barely know the meaning of the word.

■ Malcolm Gaskill is the author of *Witchcraft: A Very Short Introduction*. 978-0-19-923695-4

History

African History
John Parker
& Richard Rathbone
9780192802484

American History
Paul S. Boyer
9780195389142

American Political History
Donald Critchlow
9780199340057

American Immigration
David A. Gerber
9780195331783

American Slavery
Heather Andrea Williams
9780199922680

The American West
Stephen Aron
9780199858934

Ancient Egypt
Ian Shaw
9780192854193

Ancient Greece
Paul Cartledge
9780199601349

Ancient Near East
Amanda H. Podany
9780195377996

Ancient Warfare
Harry Sidebottom
9780192804709

The Anglo-Saxon Age
John Blair
9780192854032

Aristocracy
William Doyle
9780199206780

Archaeology
Paul Bahn
9780199657438

Australia
Kenneth Morgan
9780199589937

The Aztecs
David Carrasco
9780195379389

The British Empire
Ashley Jackson
9780199605415

The Celts
Barry Cunliffe
9780192804181

Clausewitz
Michael Howard
9780192802576

The Cold War
Robert J. McMahon
9780192801784

Colonial America
Alan Taylor
9780199766239

The Conquistadors
Matthew Restall &
Felipe Fernandez-Armesto
9780195392296

The Crusades
Christopher Tyerman
9780192806550

The Cultural Revolution
Richard Curt Kraus
9780199740550

Diaspora
Kevin Kenny
9780199858583

Druids
Barry Cunliffe
9780199539406

Eighteenth-Century Britain
Paul Langford
9780192853998

Empire
Stephen Howe
9780192802231

The Etruscans
Christopher Smith
9780199547913

Exploration
Stewart A. Weaver
978-0-19-994695-2

The First World War
Michael Howard
9780199205592

The French Revolution
William Doyle
9780192853967

Gandhi
Bhikhu Parekh
9780192854575

Global Economic History
Robert C. Allen
9780199596652

The Great Depression and New Deal
Eric Rauchway
9780195326345

Herodotus
Jennifer T. Roberts
9780199575992

History
John Arnold
9780192853523

The History of Medicine
William Bynum
9780199215430

The History of Time
Leofranc Holford-Strevens
9780192804990

Iran
Ali Ansari
9780199669349

Islamic History
Adam J. Silverstein
9780199545728

Late Antiquity
Gillian Clark
9780199546206

Lincoln
Allen C. Guelzo
9780195367805

Magna Carta
Nicholas Vincent
9780199582877

Malthus
Donald Winch
9780199670413

Mao
Delia Davin
9780199588664

Martin Luther
Scott H. Hendrix
9780199574339

Medieval Britain
John Gillingham & Ralph A. Griffiths
9780192854025

The Middle Ages
Miri Rubin
9780199697298

Modern China
Rana Mitter
9780199228027

Modern France
Vanessa Schwartz
9780195389418

Modern Ireland
Senia Paseta
9780192801678

Modern Japan
Christopher Goto-Jones
9780199235698

The Mongols
Morris Rossabi
9780199840892

Myth
Robert A. Segal
9780192803474

The Napoleonic Wars
Mike Rapport
9780199590964

Nineteenth-Century Britain
Christopher Harvie & Colin Matthew
9780192853981

The Norman Conquest
George Garnett
9780192801616

North American Indians
Theda Perdue & Michael D. Green
9780195307542

Northern Ireland
Marc Mulholland
9780192801562

The Palestinian-Israeli Conflict
Martin Bunton
9780199603930

Peace
Oliver P. Richmond
978-0-19-965600-4

The Plague
Paul Slack
9780199589548

The Reformation
Peter Marshall
9780199231317

The Renaissance
Jerry Brotton
9780192801630

Revolutions
Jack A. Goldstone
9780199858507

Roman Britain
Peter Salway
9780192854049

The Roman Empire
Christopher Kelly
9780192803917

The Roman Republic
David M. Gwynn
9780199595112

Russian History
Geoffrey Hosking
9780199580989

The Scientific Revolution
Lawrence M. Principe
9780199567416

Scotland
Rab Houston
9780199230792

The Silk Road
James A. Millward
9780199782864

The Soviet Union
Stephen Lovell
9780199238484

The Spanish Civil War
Helen Graham
9780192803771

Stuart Britain
John Morrill
9780192854001

The Russian Revolution
S. A. Smith
9780192853950

The Trojan War
Eric H. Cline
9780199760275

The Tudors
John Guy
9780199674725

Twentieth-Century Britain
Kenneth O. Morgan
9780192853974

The Vikings
Julian D. Richards
9780192806079

Voltaire
Nicholas Cronk
9780199688357

Witchcraft
Malcolm Gaskill
9780199236954

World War II
Gerhard L. Weinberg
9780199688777

Law

In this 'information age', is privacy dead?

By Raymond Wacks

Are celebrities entitled to privacy? Or do they forfeit their right? Is privacy possible online? Does the law adequately protect private lives? Should the media be more strictly controlled? What of your sensitive medical or financial data? Are they safe and secure? Has the Internet changed everything?

Newspapers are no longer the principal purveyors of news and information, and hence the publication of private facts has expanded exponentially. Blogs, Facebook, Twitter, and a myriad other outlets are available to all.

The pervasive mobile telephone fuels new privacy concerns: witness the British hacking hullabaloo of recent years. The weapon is new, but the injury is the same. It is not, of course, technology itself that is the villain, but the mischief to which it is put. Nor has our appetite for gossip diminished. A sensationalist media continues to degrade the notion of a private domain to which individuals legitimately lay claim. Celebrity is frequently regarded as a licence to intrude.

Hardly a day passes without reports of yet another onslaught on our privacy. Most conspicuously, of course, is the fragility of personal information online. But other threats generated by the digital world abound: innovations in biometrics, CCTV surveillance, radio frequency identification (RFID) systems, smart identity cards, and the manifold anti-terrorist measures all pose threats to this fundamental value—even in democratic societies.

At the same time, however, the disturbing explosion of private data through the escalation of the numerous online contrivances of our Information Age renders simple generalities about the significance of privacy problematic. Is privacy dead?

The manner in which information is collected, stored, exchanged, and used has changed forever—and, with it, the character of the threats to individual privacy. The electronic revolution touches almost every part of our lives. But is the price of the advances in technology too high? Do we remain a free society when we surrender our right to be unobserved—even when the ends are beneficial?

Although the law is a crucial instrument in the protection of privacy (and it is locked in a struggle to keep apace with the relentless advances in technology), the subject has many other dimensions: social, cultural, political, psychological, and philosophical. The concept of privacy is not easy to nail down, despite the attempts of many scholars and judges.

The courts have boldly sought to offer refuge from an increasingly intrusive media. Recent years have witnessed a deluge of civil suits by celebrities seeking to salvage what remains of their privacy. An extensive body of case law has appeared in many common law jurisdictions over the last decade. And it shows no sign of abating. For example the supermodel Naomi Campbell succeeded in the House of Lords in her claim against the *Daily Mirror* that published an article revealing her drug addiction, details of her treatment, and photographs of her outside a meeting of Narcotics Anonymous.

In Britain, the Leveson Inquiry into the culture, practice, and ethics of the press, sparked by the alleged hacking of telephones by the *News of the World*, is likely to reveal a significantly greater degree of media intrusion than is now evident. It may well propose legislative protection to buttress—or even replace—those judicial remedies fashioned by the courts.

A comprehensive privacy statute may well be the most effective solution. Carefully drafted legislation, such as exists in four Canadian provinces, would provide a remedy for intrusion and gratuitous publicity. Key elements of any such legislation should include an objective standard of liability, as well as several defences (including consent, public interest, and privilege).

Freedom of speech is, of course, no less important, and any statute will inevitably ensure that it receives explicit recognition. The two rights are often thought to be in conflict, but they are frequently complementary. How, for example, can you exercise your right to free speech when your telephone is hacked or your email messages intercepted?

Privacy is accorded superior safeguards in Europe than in the United States, which has still to acknowledge the inadequacy of its reliance on the Supreme Court to protect privacy against an escalating digital onslaught. Much of its common law privacy protection is based on the Fourth Amendment to the Constitution which protects the right of the people 'to be secure in their persons, houses, papers, and effects, against unreasonable searches and seizures'. It would be more effective if the government were to ratify the Council of Europe Privacy Convention. This would mark a significant step towards safeguarding this rapidly eroding right. The United States lags far behind the more than 50 countries with comprehensive data protection legislation. It surely cannot continue to seek 18th century remedies to 21st century challenges.

In the case of film stars, models, pop stars, and other public figures, it seems that our—frequently lurid—interest in their private lives spawns a thirst for intimate facts which many tabloids are more than willing to satisfy.

■ Raymond Wacks is the author of *Privacy: A Very Short Introduction*. 978-0-19-955653-3

Law

American Legal History
G. Edward White
9780199766000

Family Law
Jonathan Herring
9780199668526

Human Rights
Andrew Clapham
9780199205523

Law
Raymond Wacks
9780199214969

Medical Law
Charles Foster
9780199660445

Philosophy of Law
Raymond Wacks
9780199687008

Privacy
Raymond Wacks
9780199556533

The U.S. Supreme Court
Linda Greenhouse
9780199754540

Philosophy

Derrida and Europe beyond Eurocentrism and anti-Eurocentrism

By Simon Glendinning

Two months before his death in October 2004, Jacques Derrida gave an interview to the French newspaper *Le Monde* which turned out to be his last. Although he refused to treat it as an occasion in which to give what he called 'a health bulletin', he acknowledged that he was seriously ill, and the discussion is overshadowed by that fact: there is a strong sense of someone taking stock, someone taking the chance to give a final word.

In this context, what is so striking about the interview is not the wide range of topics that he covered—that was typical—but the extent to which Europe came to frame so many of his remarks on them.

Europe had been the theme of an analysis by Derrida in a text entitled 'The Other Heading: Reflections on Today's Europe', written in 1991—written, then, as Europe was celebrating a 'reunion' after the fall of the Berlin Wall and the end of Soviet communism. However, in the final interview Derrida drew his work as a whole into a European context, and he highlighted the extent to which his work was run through by critical reflections on what he called 'Eurocentrism'.

Eurocentrism can be defined as that attitude which regards European culture and civilization as superior to every other. It expresses a kind of uncritical and narcissistic self-love, self-congratulation, and celebratory back-slapping. For a Eurocentric thinker Europe is not just one sample of human culture among others, not just one regional culture among others—but is the best example, the head of the pack: the avant-garde for the whole of humanity in its history and its development.

In his very early writings Derrida had tended to say his target was an 'ethnocentric' discourse, but as his work developed he more and more came to refer to it as 'Eurocentric'. In the last interview he states that 'since the beginning of my work . . . I have remained very critical with regard to Eurocentrism . . . Deconstruction in general is a project that many have taken, rightly so, as an act of defiance toward all Eurocentrism.' Derrida even says that this act of defiance 'is deconstruction itself'.

This fact is both what marks the abiding significance of deconstruction—and what led it on a path of near disaster. In the hands of a largely academic readership that was increasingly hostile to Europe's global legacy, and wanted nothing more to do with the Dead White European Males whose work had dominated the university curriculum, deconstruction became a new buzzword for rejecting the European heritage, for condemning everything European.

It was in this cultural cauldron that Derrida became the *bête noire* for anyone who retained a devoted interest in the classic canon of European thought; and became the new voice of defiance for a generation of academics who wanted to reject it—and who now had new words with which to do so: the European heritage could now be denounced as 'logocentric', 'ethnocentric', 'phonocentric', 'phallogocentric', or 'Eurocentric'.

However, while Derrida was indeed defiantly critical of Eurocentrism, he did not write, as he put it, in a 'critical fury' against the European heritage, but rather for the sake of that heritage, out of love for it, concerned above all to forge a future for it—but, yes, yes, a future beyond its dominant Eurocentrism. The point is that deconstruction was never a form of anti-Eurocentrism: it did not set out to condemn Europe or to replace

Eurocentric self-love with anti-Eurocentric self-loathing. His claim was not that the great texts of the European heritage are finished—but precisely that they are not: there is more to be read, more to be thought. These great texts—in the final interview he mentions a line running from Plato, the Bible, to Kant, Marx, Freud, Heidegger, and beyond—still lie ahead of us and remain to be read. Derrida did not just want to open a path for thinking 'beyond Eurocentrism'—but, equally, 'beyond anti-Eurocentrism' too.

Crucially this 'beyond' was not thought of as a movement that would simply break with the European tradition. On the contrary, this capacity to 'break with itself' was affirmed as precisely internal to that tradition—and hence the work of self-critique that Derrida undertook in the name of deconstruction was something he understood as a way of being faithful to Europe's heritage. In the last interview, Derrida put it like this:

> Since the days of the Enlightenment, Europe has been in a permanent state of self-critique, and in this tradition of perfectibility there is a hope for the future. At least I hope so, and this is what fuels my indignation before utterances that condemn Europe utterly, as if it were defined only by its crimes.

This European legacy of responsible and relentless self-critique is what Derrida wanted to save, to preserve, and to radicalize. In my view, Derrida is among those who should count most for us today—among those for whom the idea that we have finally done with the question of how to live is experienced most intensely, most keenly, as something—today—to resist.

■ Simon Glendinning is the author of *Derrida: A Very Short Introduction*. 978-0-19-280345-0

What is the probability that you are dreaming right now?

By Jan Westerhoff

Most people think that even though it is possible that they are dreaming right now, the probability of this is very small, perhaps as small as winning the lottery or being struck by lightning. In fact the probability is quite high. Let's do the maths.

Assume your life is made up of a finite number of moments of consciousness (we'll call these mocs). For the sake of simplicity let there be one moc per second. If we get a healthy 8 hours of sleep every night we are left with 16 hours = 57,600 mocs that constitute our waking time. Every night we are asleep for 2,880 seconds. We know that 20 to 25 per cent of our sleep consists of REM sleep, the kind of sleep during which dreaming takes place. Assuming the lower figure of 20 per cent, this leaves us with 5,760 mocs, while we are dreaming. So 1 out of every 10 mocs happens during a dream; the odds that your current moc is one of them is one in ten.

But is it reasonable to assume that there are moments of consciousness outside of the waking state? Norman Malcolm argued in 1956 that this was logically impossible, claiming that 'if a person is in any state of consciousness it logically follows that he is not sound asleep'. But whether there is consciousness in dreams appears to depend entirely on what we take consciousness to be. We can hardly claim that a consensus on this has been reached, but if we understand consciousness in accordance with the contemporary discussion as something that can come in different strengths and constitutes at the very least an appearance of a world then dreams do constitute some form for consciousness, since in a dream some form of a world appears to us.

But even if dreams are conscious experiences we might think the above argument is a bit too quick. As experience confirms, one hour of carrying out a habitual, boring task does not equal 3,600 mocs; our consciousness might be elsewhere for most of the time. Moreover, time in dreams might not obey the rules of the waking world, a dream-second may correspond to fewer or more mocs than a waking-second. This is true, but if we spend more of our waking life unconscious the ratio of waking mocs to dreaming mocs increases. It becomes even more likely that your present moment of consciousness happens during a dream.

How dream-time relates to waking-time is indeed a difficult question. Sequences of events that take days can flash by in an hour's dream; when you are dreaming, a lot can happen in a short time. Nevertheless we should note that as far as we can empirically determine the relation between dream-time and waking-time the two seem to be running at the same speed. Sleep researchers came up with a very clever way of testing this. Since the movement of our eyes is the only bodily action we can control during dreaming, experiments could be carried out with lucid dreamers asked to signal the beginning and end of an estimated time period by moving their eyes. These signals could then be tracked in a sleep laboratory. The average length of an estimated 10-second interval of dream-time was 13 seconds of waking time, which is the same as the average length of an estimated 10-second interval of waking time. If this fact about lucid dreams can be generalized it seems to be the case that there is the same amount of moments of consciousness per unit of time during the waking state as there is in a dream.

Now a 10 per cent likelihood appears quite high. We usually regard the possibility that we are dreaming right now as something that is logically possible, but highly unlikely, in other words as an event with probability of significantly less than 0.1 per cent. Of course none of the above claims that we can never be more than 90 per cent certain that we are presently not dreaming. We could, for example, employ some sort of reality-testing techniques to find out whether we are really dreaming. (Two techniques recommended by sleep researchers involve trying to jump into the air to check whether we stay airborne any longer than usual, and looking at a piece of printed text twice to see whether the letters have changed). But it is not quite clear how the outcomes of these experiments should influence our credence. It is possible that they deliver a negative outcome (we fall to the ground immediately, the text stays constant) but we are still dreaming. Moreover, the very fact that we feel the need to carry out a reality test may be a strong indication that we are dreaming. Philosophy tutorials aside, when we are awake we rarely wonder whether we are really awake.

■ Jan Westerhoff is the author of *Reality: A Very Short Introduction*. 978-0-19-959441-2

Thought control

Tim Bayne

As a teacher I have sometimes offered a million pounds to any student who can form any one of the following beliefs: that they can fly; that they were born on the moon; or that sheep are carnivorous. Needless to say, I have never had to pay up. The Queen in Lewis Carroll's *Through the Looking Glass* might have been able to believe six impossible things before breakfast, but that is a feat few of us can match. In fact, it is doubtful whether the formation of belief is under voluntary control at all. Adopting a belief seems to be more like digesting or metabolizing, and rather unlike looking or speaking—it seems to be something that happens to one rather than something that one does.

But unlike digestion or metabolizing, the upshot of belief-formation has a direct impact on how we behave. Although we don't always act in accordance with our beliefs, it goes without saying that what we believe plays a huge role in governing what we do. More importantly, a rational person ought to act on the basis of their beliefs; indeed, failing to act in light of one's beliefs is a form of irrationality.

In and of themselves the two claims that we have just examined—that belief-formation is involuntary and that a person's beliefs justify their actions—are unobjectionable. Trouble looms, however, when we put them together. From Francisco Pizarro to Tomás de Torquemada, and from Khalid Sheikh Mohammed to Anders Breivik, history is littered with the carnage wrought by the actions of sincere but misguided individuals—people who have regarded the superiority of their religion, race, or ideology as legitimizing actions that we regard as horrific.

How should we regard such individuals? If the formation of belief is involuntary, then, one might think, we cannot justifiably condemn them for holding the beliefs that motivated their actions. Can we condemn them for acting on those beliefs? Arguably not, for how else is a person to act if not on the basis of their beliefs? But if we cannot condemn them either for forming their beliefs or for acting in light of their beliefs, what grounds do we have for condemning them at all?

Some might be tempted to respond that we don't have any grounds for condemning such individuals, and that those who act on the basis of their sincerely held beliefs shouldn't be denounced for what they do, no matter how awful their deeds. We could, of course, continue to regard such agents as legally responsible for their crimes, but—according to this line of thought—we have no grounds for holding them morally guilty for the actions that they carry out in light of their convictions.

Although some might be happy to settle for this solution, I suspect that for many of us it is a response of last resort—a position to be adopted only when all other avenues are exhausted. Are there any other avenues available to us?

Perhaps we were too quick to embrace the idea that belief-formation is always involuntary. Although it is clear that we cannot simply decide to adopt any old proposition that is put to us, it doesn't follow—and it may not be true—that we have no intentional control over what we believe. For example, it is surely plausible to suppose that we have some control over whether or not to subject our beliefs to critical scrutiny. One can deliberate about whether or not to believe those propositions that are open questions for one. And if deliberation lies within one's voluntary control, then perhaps one can be justifiably blamed for failing to deliberate appropriately.

Perhaps so, but does this solve our puzzle? I suspect not. For one thing, I very much doubt whether the beliefs that motivated Khalid Sheikh Mohammed and Anders Breivik were 'open questions' from their point of view. Instead, I suspect that they regarded them as self-evident truths, claims no more deserving of critical scrutiny than the belief that 2+2=4 or the belief that there is water at the bottom of the ocean. Moreover, even if they were guilty of failing to subject their beliefs to the kind of scrutiny that they should have, that failing would surely be relatively minor rather than an instance of gross moral turpitude of the kind for which we are inclined to hold them guilty.

So, how should we resolve this puzzle? I don't have a full solution to offer, but here is one line of thought that I find tempting. Although belief-formation is responsive to evidence, it is also influenced by desire and motivation: how we take the world to be is heavily influenced by how we would like the world to be. And one of the central sources of belief in the superiority of one's religion, race, or ideology is surely the desire to dominate one's fellow human beings.

And here, perhaps, we can see the hint of a solution to our puzzle. What the Khalid Sheikh Mohammeds and Anders Breiviks of this world are guilty of is not the fact that they have voluntarily adopted unjustified beliefs, for we have seen that it is doubtful whether their beliefs were voluntarily acquired. Rather, their guilt lies in the character traits that their beliefs manifest. Our condemnation of them is justified insofar as the beliefs that motivated their actions were grounded in intolerance, arrogance, and self-aggrandizement.

■ Tim Bayne is the author of *Thought: A Very Short Introduction*.
  978-0-19-960172-1

Can ignorance ever be an excuse?

By Katherine Hawley

We have developed quite a taste for chastising the mighty in public. In place of rotten fruit and stocks, we now have Leveson, Chilcot, and the parliamentary select committees which have cross-examined Bob Diamond of Barclays and Nick Buckles of G4S.

Diamond and Buckles, Tony Blair and James Murdoch: all have been asked to account for acknowledged mistakes and wrong-doing in their organizations, from rate-fixing to phone-hacking, via the mysterious dearth of both Olympic security guards and Iraqi weapons of mass destruction. All have professed themselves shocked—shocked!—when the problems came to light. Murdoch notoriously does not recall crucial meetings and communications, Diamond was 'physically ill' when he discovered along with the rest of us that his underlings had been fiddling the Libor, whilst for Buckles it was a 'complete and utter shock' to discover only three weeks before the Olympics that his company had failed to recruit enough guards, despite signing the security contract years earlier.

Are these professions of ignorance genuine? It's hard to be sure, although both Chilcot and Leveson have laboured to establish who knew what, and when; who saw which email or unredacted report; who attended which unminuted meeting.

It matters who knew what, and when. But does it really matter?

These are all powerful men, extravagantly well-paid (though Blair has reaped his primary financial rewards only since leaving office). Never mind whether they actually knew what was going on. It was their job to know!

At the heart of these enquiries, cross-examinations, and chastisements lie issues of trust and distrust, trustworthiness and untrustworthiness. When we trust, we take risks along two different dimensions. We trust in the sincerity and honesty of others, and we

59

also trust in their skills, knowledge, and competence. Failure along either of these dimensions is enough to trigger distrust: you cannot trust someone you take to be dishonest, but neither can you trust someone you take to be incompetent.

Just as trust has two dimensions, so does trustworthiness. Trustworthy people are sincere, for sure. But sincerity isn't enough. We all have friends or colleagues who are ready to volunteer help or opinions at the drop of a hat, all with the very best intentions, yet rarely seem capable of following through on these offers, or coming up with genuinely reliable information. Along with sincerity, trustworthy people also need the skills and knowledge to make good on their promises.

Too harsh? Trustworthiness is a prized moral virtue. Is it really achievable only by those who have developed complex skills, studied for higher degrees, or memorized the *Oxford English Dictionary*? No. You can be trustworthy without doing all this, so long as you have a decent idea of your own limitations, and don't make commitments which take you wildly beyond those limitations. Self-knowledge is crucial.

In our personal relationships, we often find it easier to forgive those who let us down through error and incompetence than to forgive those who deliberately mislead us or make promises they have no intention of keeping. Still, we are wary of those well-meaning people who repeatedly let us down, and we become reluctant to trust them, even if we are inclined to understand a little more and condemn a little less than we do with blatant liars.

But matters are different for Murdoch, Diamond, and their ilk. They did not simply find themselves in charge of complex organizations; they volunteered for these jobs, knowing the demands of the roles. In offering themselves up for these positions, they took responsibility for their own trustworthiness in carrying them out: sincerity and good intentions are not enough, if competence and knowledge are missing. Again, frank self-knowledge is crucial.

Is it reasonable to expect one man to know the details of every corner of the organization he leads? No. But it is reasonable to expect structures of reporting and review designed to bring systematic problems to the attention of those at the top. And it is reasonable to expect huge corporate salaries to buy some accountability from those who receive them. Ignorance is not an excuse.

■ Katherine Hawley is the author of *Trust: A Very Short Introduction*.
978-0-19-969734-2

Philosophy

Ancient Philosophy
Julia Annas
9780192853578

Animal Rights
David DeGrazia
9780192853608

Thomas Aquinas
Fergus Kerr
9780199556649

Aristotle
Jonathan Barnes
9780192854087

Atheism
Julian Baggini
9780192804242

Barthes
Jonathan Culler
9780192801593

Beauty
Roger Scruton
9780199229758

Causation
Stephen Mumford and
Rani Lill Anjum
9780199684434

Choice Theory
Michael Allingham
9780192803030

Confucianism
Daniel K. Gardner
9780195398915

Conscience
Paul Strohm
9780199569694

Continental Philosophy
Simon Critchley
9780192853592

Critical Theory
Stephen Eric Bronner
9780199730070

Derrida
Simon Glendinning
9780192803450

Descartes
Tom Sorell
9780192854094

Emotion
Dylan Evans
9780192804617

Ethics
Simon Blackburn
9780192804426

Existentialism
Thomas Flynn
9780192804280

Foucault
Gary Gutting
9780192805577

Free Speech
Nigel Warburton
9780199232352

Free Will
Thomas Pink
9780192853585

Genius
Andrew Robinson
9780199594405

German Philosophy
Andrew Bowie
9780199569250

Habermas
James Gordon Finlayson
9780192840950

Happiness
Daniel M. Haybron
9780199590605

Hegel
Peter Singer
9780192801975

Heidegger
Michael Inwood
9780192854100

Can ignorance ever be an excuse?

Hobbes
Richard Tuck
9780192802552

Humanism
Stephen Law
9780199553648

Hume
A. J. Ayer
9780192854063

Humour
Noël Carroll
9780199552221

Ideology
Michael Freeden
9780192802811

Indian Philosophy
Sue Hamilton
9780192853745

Kant
Roger Scruton
9780192801999

Kierkegaard
Patrick Gardiner
9780192802569

Knowledge
Jennifer Nagel
9780199661268

Locke
John Dunn
9780192803948

Logic
Graham Priest
9780192893208

The Meaning of Life
Terry Eagleton
9780199532179

Metaphysics
Stephen Mumford
9780199657124

Nietzsche
Michael Tanner
9780192854148

Objectivity
Stephen Gaukroger
9780199606696

Philosophy
Edward Craig
9780192854216

Philosophy of Law
Raymond Wacks
9780199687008

Philosophy of Science
Samir Okasha
9780192802835

Plato
Julia Annas
9780192802163

Political Philosophy
David Miller
9780192803955

Presocratic Philosophy
Catherine Osborne
9780192840943

Reality
Jan Westerhoff
9780199594412

Rousseau
Robert Wokler
9780192801982

Russell
A. C. Grayling
9780192802583

Schopenhauer
Christopher Janaway
9780192802590

Socrates
Christopher Taylor
9780192854124

Spinoza
Roger Scruton
9780192803160

Thought
Tim Bayne
9780199601721

Trust
Katherine Hawley
9780199697342

Utopianism
Lyman Tower Sargent
9780199573400

Voltaire
Nicholas Cronk
9780199688357

Wittgenstein
A. C. Grayling
9780192854117

Politics

Putting Syria in its place

By Klaus Dodds

Where exactly is Syria, and how is Syria represented as a place? The first part of the question might appear to be fairly straight forward. Syria is an independent state in western Asia and borders Lebanon, Turkey, Jordan, and Israel. It occupies an area of approximately 70,000 square miles, which is similar in size to the state of North Dakota. Before the civil war (March 2011 onwards), the population was estimated to be around 23 million, but millions of people have been displaced by the crisis. We must also add into the equation that around 18 million other people living in North America, Latin America, Europe, and Australia are of Syrian descent. Famous people of Syrian descent include the late Steve Jobs of Apple fame and the actress Teri Hatcher. So where does Syria begin and end when we factor in the Syrian diaspora?

How has Syria been understood as a place?

During the ongoing and bloody civil war, we have arguably been bombarded with news stories and images of a country that has rarely enjoyed such prominence. Fundamentally, and over a period of 18 months, Syria transformed from a minor element of Middle Eastern geopolitics (compared to Israel, Iran, and Palestine in the past) and Arab Spring transformation (compared to Egypt, Tunisia, and Libya) to a place of mass concern. But making sense of the Syrian civil war or uprising remains a deeply contested affair, as rival groups inside and outside Syria struggle to frame Syria in political and geographical terms. My contention is that Syria can be understood in six fundamental and, at times, competing ways.

1. *Syria represented as a place of humanitarian disaster*

The ongoing conflict in Syria has uprooted communities and forced millions to flee across international borders, or seek safety within the country as internally displaced people. The United Nations (UN) believes that around 40 per cent of the population requires humanitarian assistance and some six million people are thought to be displaced in some fashion. As a space of unfolding and continued humanitarian disaster, Syria becomes increasingly demanding of our attention: the focus of concern and assistance in the wake of worries that the state is no longer able to function in a way that is conducive to the security of its citizens. As a humanitarian disaster, it also heightened the likelihood that Syria's territorial sovereignty will need to be violated in order for the UN and others to offer protection and support for vulnerable citizens, many of whom are women, children, and the elderly.

2. *Syria framed as a space of extremism*

The civil war is believed to have unleashed new forces of extremism and sectarianism. Syria in the process becomes a more complex place. Maps circulate purporting to show the ethnic composition of the country, and like maps of the former Yugoslavia and Iraq, they help to sustain arguments warning of long-standing animosities and dangers facing those who intervene. It becomes an opportunity for others to note that Syria is an 'invented country'; a product of the First World War and the French mandate. As if to suggest, as a consequence, 'what do you expect?' Extremism flourishes in such complexity where the ruling elite are a minority sect of Islam (Alawites).

3. *Syria represented as a place of opportunity*

The 'big powers' and 'rising powers' that are using Syria opportunistically play out their own agenda so that less attention is given to Syria as a complex inhabited place. Syria becomes both a stage and a conduit for diplomatic and military performances, and a space for flows of arms and other forms of support to particular factions. Some of the players, such as Qatar, are relatively new to this kind of 'big power geopolitics', but apparently driven by a desire to be seen as a more active geopolitical agent in the region. Others, such as Russia, have had a long-standing relationship with the Syrian regime and consider the country to be strategically significant, close to the Mediterranean, and close to oil and gas fields of the Middle East. A view that, it is argued, the US shares as well.

4. *Syria framed as a place ruled by conspiracy*

The fourth version of Syria addresses its role as a place of and for conspiracy. The crisis is thus seen as a 'distraction' from what is really happening with commentators keen to point out antecedents; for example, the theory that Syria is part of a wider plot by the US to weaken both Iran and its close ally Syria along with its ally Hezbollah in Lebanon. Other stories include the UK government under Tony Blair considering anti-Syrian activity, in alliance with the United States, because of fears that Syria was not reliable when it came to protecting Western hydrocarbon interests, including a pipeline deal involving Iran and Iraq. Conspiracy theorizing, which is hugely popular in the Middle East, has become an alternative way of viewing places like Syria, where the focus is less on 'appearances' and more on detecting 'hidden' aspects such as discovering secret meetings, covert operations, and sensitive documents.

5. *Syria as a 'leaky container', a space with insecure borders and a place barely able to contain flows of people, arms and ideas*

The most notable example of this instance is Lebanon, where the Syrian civil war has stretched across an international border and affected the political life of communities there. In November 2013, a bombing occurred outside the Iranian Embassy in Beirut killing 23, and this was attributed to a group, the Abdullah Azzam Shaheed Brigade, who are in opposition to the Syrian regime. This followed months of violence in Lebanese cities and towns such as Beirut, Sidon, and Tripoli. But, it is worth bearing in mind that this spill-over is not just one way. Syria, in the recent past, has also been a space of hospitality as spill-over from the Iraqi crisis which has resulted in over 1.5 million people fleeing over the Iraqi-Syrian border. Spill-over has also caused anxiety to other neighbours, such as Jordan, who fear that more refugees will arrive from Syria.

6. *Syria as a place indicative of international norms*

In this instance Syria becomes a testing place; a place where the international community must 'prove' itself. The bleak stories regarding the use of chemical weapons against civilian populations in August 2013 became a moment to act, not only because of civilian suffering, but because an international norm had been violated. So in principle, the place in question is irrelevant. President Obama, for example, was swift to draw attention to the violation of such norms, and to warn that a failure to act might lead to increased risk of future usage of chemical weapons. The violation of the norm not only presents a danger in the here and now, it also points to future dangers that can now be increasingly imagined as a consequence of the attacks in August 2013. While calls for military strikes were later called off as a consequence of high-level US–Russian diplomacy, Syria remains 'testing', not only of international cooperation, but also in terms of whether it can be proven that weapons of mass destruction have been safely secured. It also became a moment, repeatedly, for 'Syria' to be invoked as emblematic of the limits of the United Nations and the role of obstructive others.

■ **Klaus Dodds is the author of** *Geopolitics: A Very Short Introduction*. **978-0-19-967678-1**

Globalization:
Q&A with Manfred Steger

How has globalization changed in the last ten years? We asked Manfred Steger, author of *Globalization: A Very Short Introduction*, how he felt it has been affected by world events in the decade since the first edition of his Very Short Introduction was published.

1. The VSI is now in its third edition. What have been the most important/significant changes in globalization since the first edition in 2003?

The most important change is the addition of a substantive chapter on the 'ecological dimensions of globalization', which discusses global climate change and the global impact of major environmental disasters such as the destruction of the Fukushima nuclear reactor in the wake of the 2011 earthquake, and the 2010 BP gulf oil spill. Also the chapter on the 'ideological dimensions of globalization' has been further developed and expanded. It now introduces three different types of 'globalisms'. Finally, the opening chapter explains the basic concepts of globalization in the context of the 2010 Football World Cup in South Africa. Of course, all the other chapters have been updated and revised to engage current issues.

2. Social networking has become a large part of everyday life for many people. How has this changed globalization in a cultural context?

Social networking has intensified cultural globalization by increasing cultural flows across the world. Some experts argue that the global standardization of the Facebook or Twitter templates has increased cultural tendencies of homogenization (or 'Americanization'), whereas other scholars emphasize the creation and proliferation of new (sub-cultures) as a result of social networking. My own perspective is that social networking also contributes to cultural 'hybridization'—the mixing up of different cultural values, styles, and preferences resulting in new cultural expressions that blur the line between 'Western' and 'non-Western' cultural formations.

3. How do you see the state of globalization in five years' time?

Unless there is another major global crisis that surpasses the 2008 Global Financial Crisis, I believe that globalization dynamics will further intensify. With the ICT revolution still in full swing, we can expect in five years' time the emergence of new communication devices that are not even imaginable today. But I am not particularly enthusiastic about the intensifying digitalization of social relationships. The dark side of this dynamic is the decline of face-to-face interactions and physical contact—two basic human qualities that foster a strong sense of community among people.

4. How would you respond to claims that globalization is ideological?

As I point out in my book, globalization always has ideological dimensions. There is no such thing as a neutral, unbiased perspective on something as multi-faceted and contentious as globalization. At the moment the three main ideological forces employ different types of 'globalisms'—ideologies centred on globalization—to convince their global audiences of the superiority of their respective political and social views. I call these ideologies 'market globalism' (neoliberalism), 'justice globalism', and 'religious globalism'. The neoliberal worldview is still the strongest, but has come under attack, especially in the wake of the 2008 Global Financial Crisis.

5. In economic terms, can globalization benefit all, or will it only benefit high earners?

It depends what form of globalization we are talking about. Market-led globalization, for example, claims that, in the long run, globalization—understood as the liberalization and global integration of markets—will benefit all. But a recent major study undertaken by Branko Milanović, the leading economist at the World Bank, shows that the bottom 5 per cent of the world population has not benefitted at all in more than two decades of market-led globalization. Of course, there have also been improvements in global South countries like China and India, but the economic benefits have disproportionately gone to those at the top income bracket. I think it is important to develop more ethical forms of globalization aimed at reducing the growing inequality gap within and among nations. Fortunately, more world leaders have become aware of the rising tide of social and economic inequality. Pope Francis, for example, issued a powerful encyclical that warns us of the dangers of growing worldwide disparities in wealth and well-being.

6. Do you think the subject should be covered more in schools?

I do. In universities around the world, there are currently strong efforts underway to further expand the growing transdisciplinary field of global studies, which focuses on the exploration of the many dimensions of globalization. But the basics of globalization should be taught as early as primary school and most certainly in secondary school. Unfortunately, many current lesson plans require serious updating to engage the major global issues (and problems) of our global age.

7. Has the financial crisis paused the progress of globalization?

The momentum of market globalism was slowed down in response to the economic crash of 2008 and the ensuing Great Recession. But those market globalist ideas of the 'Roaring 1990s' and 2000s are still tremendously influential—as we can see in ongoing attempts by neoliberal governments around the world to cut taxes, restrict spending, deregulate the economy, and privatize the few remaining public industries.

8. Are there any environmental costs of globalization (increased international trade etc.)?

The environmental costs to market-led globalization have been horrific. That is why the 3rd edition of my VSI contains such a substantive chapter on this topic. I believe that the deteriorating ecological health of our planet will become the most pressing global problem by mid century at the latest. We simply can no longer afford business-as-usual. The problem is not just global warming, but various forms of transboundary pollution (such as the staggering amount of trash and plastics that find their way into our planet's soil and oceans) and the rapid decline of biodiversity. And if we don't switch from fossil fuels to alternative forms of clean energy any time soon, we will reach our ecological point of no return.

9. What is the most exciting/innovative research going on in global studies at the moment?

Political geographers and urban studies scholars have been contributing highly innovative approaches to the study of globalization. Their emphasis on theorizing space is a much-needed corrective to the conceptual frameworks of those of us who have been trained to focus primarily on the role of language, ideas, and economics in evolution of human societies. Obviously, the compression of space and time is at the heart of globalization, so it behoves us to pay closer attention to the current reconfigurations of spatial arrangements, especially in the context of our expanding 'global cities' and the loss of areas of wilderness.

10. If you weren't a political science academic, what would you be?

I am fascinated by the history and culture of ancient Rome, so perhaps I would be a classicist or a historian of the Roman Empire. Or, even better, a bestselling author of historical novels!

■ Manfred B. Steger is the author of *Globalization: A Very Short Introduction*. 978-0-19-966266-1

What have we learned from modern wars?

By Richard English

War remains arguably the greatest threat that we face as a species. It also remains an area of activity in which we still tend to get far too many things wrong. For there's a depressing disjunction between what we very often assume, think, expect, and claim about modern war, and its actual historical reality when carefully assessed. The alleged causes for wars beginning and ending often fail to match the actual reasons behind these developments; meanwhile, the things making people actually fight in such wars often differ both from the ostensible claims made by or about such warriors, and also from the actual reasons for the wars occurring in any case. Much of what we anticipate, celebrate, commemorate, and remember regarding the experience and achievements of modern war bears only partially overlapping relation to historical reality, and wars' actual achievements greatly diverge from both the publicly articulated and the actual aims and justifications behind their initial eruption. Again—and most depressingly—most of our attempts to set out prophylactic measures and structures against modern war have seemed (and continue to appear) frequently doomed to blood-spattered failure.

Consider some of the conflicts likely to dominate memory of the first years of the 21st century. The Iraq War which began in 2003 was publicly justified on various grounds, including the false claim that Saddam Hussein had played a role in generating the 9/11 atrocity; the mistaken assertion that he possessed a certain array of weapons of mass destruction and thus represented an immediate threat to the West; and the claim that his regime was vile and oppressive—itself a reasonable point, but one undermined by the fact that the USA and its allies have tolerated in the past, and continue to tolerate in the present, equally or more despicable regimes remaining in power when political judgement seems to recommend such an approach.

In the event, the early phase of the Iraq War saw a dramatic and impressive military victory for the US-led campaign. But this was followed by a postwar phase of appalling violence, ill-considered policy, political chaos, and hubristic assertions about victory. The casting of the Iraq War as part of a War on Terror made it even less persuasive as a venture. There were, perhaps, some sound reasons for wanting to depose Saddam Hussein (among them, the view that he indeed did want to possess weapons of mass destruction, and that it would be better to depose him before rather than after he had acquired them). But in terms of terrorism, what Iraq did was to intensify the desire of some people to attack Western forces—whether in Iraq itself or in Western countries. And it is likely that, in a hundred years' time, very few people will be able to name even a handful of victims of early-21st century al-Qaida terrorism, but that many people will remember the lesser nastiness of Abu Ghraib prison, and the unnecessary discrediting of the USA as a consequence.

My suspicion is that we will fail to learn very much, in terms of future political planning, from these mistakes and difficulties. Has the USA and UK sounded much more persuasive, and seemed more sure-footed, in their reaction to the varied conflicts emerging recently in Libya, Syria, or Egypt? Did the ludicrous over-reaction of the authorities in Boston to the terrible (but ultimately trivial, in terms of its global, political weight) marathon bombing suggest that we have moved forward in how we respond to what has tended to be very small terrorist threats?

It is possible, as scholars such as Harvard's Steven Pinker have powerfully argued, that we are becoming less violent overall as a species, in terms of the percentage likelihood of members of the human race actually experiencing violent actions. It is also true, however, that our tendency to misdiagnose causes, to anticipate futures which do not have much chance in practice of occurring, to present dubious justifications for naively sanctioned campaigns of warfare, and to over-react to small provocations by terrorist groups and individuals, might yet produce certain explosive conflicts which carry with them truly devastating consequences— consequences likely to endure far longer than the short-term and unhistorical thinking which brought them into being.

- ■ Richard English is the author of *Modern War: A Very Short Introduction*. 978-0-19-960789-1

Global warfare *redivivus*

By Charles Townshend

When the 'global war on terror' was launched by George W. Bush—closely followed by Tony Blair—after the 9/11 attacks, many people no doubt felt reassured by these leaders' confidence that they knew the best way to retaliate. Some, though, found the global war concept alarming for several reasons. The notion of a 'war' seemed to indicate a wrong-headed belief that overt military action, rather than secret intelligence methods, was an effective response. More seriously, perhaps, this seemed to be a 'war' which couldn't be won. Since it is all but inconceivable that terrorism *per se* can ever be eliminated by any method, the Bush-Blair crusade looked dangerously like a declaration of permanent war of an Orwellian kind.

If by chance Bush and Blair had misread the threat posed by terrorism, they might be using a sledgehammer to crack a nut which would be not just financially wasteful but politically damaging if (as was inevitable) force was sometimes used against the wrong targets. The collateral damage of the invasions of Afghanistan and Iraq showed such apprehensions to be well founded. Incredibly—from the Bush-Blair standpoint—some security experts would come to the conclusion ten years on that the military interventions had increased rather than diminished the threat of terrorism.

So how was that threat read? In almost apocalyptic terms, the terrorists were said to be driven by mortal hatred of the West and to represent a deadly threat to 'our way of life'. The first assertion was true as far as it went; the second, a patent exaggeration, but one which went largely unchallenged and unexamined. British journalists showed remarkably little inclination to press ministers to explain its logic. (As, for instance, when the Chancellor of the Exchequer allocated £3 billion in the 2003 budget to cover the cost of Britain's part in the invasion of Iraq—a figure that even then was clearly a wildly optimistic estimate). It took the passage of nearly a decade, including two fearsomely expensive, destructive, and ineffective 'real wars', to undermine it. And it was not a politician but a judge who first pointed out the absurdity of trying to set the threat posed to 'our way of life' by terrorist groups on the same level as that posed by the Wehrmacht in 1940.

At last, the Foreign Secretary David Miliband broke ranks and accepted that the concept of the war on terror was 'misleading and mistaken'. Worryingly late in the day, perhaps, but better late than never. The spectre of an unending war seemed to be laid to rest. Miliband specifically criticized the notion of a 'unified transnational enemy' that had been evoked in the global war on terror. He had grasped that al-Qaida had not lived up to its billing.

So it came as something of a surprise when David Cameron, who had seemed unconcerned to take up this element of the Blair legacy, reacted to the January 2013 attack on the Amenas gas plant in southern Algeria by pronouncing it part of a 'global threat'. This grim event in the deepest Sahara desert was the work of an extremist Islamist terrorist group linked, like those in Pakistan and Afghanistan, to al-Qaida, whose aim, the Prime Minister held, was 'to destroy our way of life'.

If his intention was to counter the risk that the public might dismiss the attack as too distant to be worth serious consideration, fair enough. But the terms he used surely went beyond what was needed for that. He went as far as to label the threat represented by the terrorists 'existential'. This striking echo of 2001 did not go entirely unchallenged, as it had done a decade previously. This time, journalists with real experience like Jason Burke are around to point out that al-Qaida, reeling from 'blow after blow' over the last five years, is only a shadow of the organization that once did perhaps represent a threat on a global scale. And that, however deadly the Amenas attack, 'a gas refinery in southern Algeria is not the Pentagon'.

But clearly such perspectives (shared, as Burke pointed out, by the Prime Minister's security experts) do not meet the rhetorical needs of the moment. David Miliband's key argument was that the more we lump terrorist groups together and draw the battle lines as a simple binary struggle between moderates and extremists, 'the more we play into the hands of those seeking to unify groups with little in common'. What seemed by 2009 to have become no more than common sense has now been peremptorily abandoned again.

Jason Burke, maybe too charitably, described Cameron's rhetoric as 'dated'. That would in itself not be reassuring, but there seems to be something more going on. Though he specifically rejected the idea of a purely military solution, the Prime Minister's emphasis on the 'ungoverned spaces' in which terrorists thrive opens up an agenda at least as indefinite as the original war on terror. His undertaking to 'close down' such spaces, and acceptance that this would take decades, has revived the spectre of a protracted conflict without proposing any plausible method of ending it. The function of these 'ungoverned spaces' is in fact highly doubtful. If such spaces exist—and the concept is highly disputable—they may well be useful to terrorist groups, but to suggest that they are crucial is seriously misleading. The fact that the deadliest Islamist attack in Britain was carried out by people from Leeds, Huddersfield, and Aylesbury might of course indicate that Yorkshire and Buckinghamshire are also 'ungoverned spaces', but the implications of that would be alarming indeed.

■ Charles Townshend is the author of *Terrorism: A Very Short Introduction*. 978-0-19-960394-7

Politics

American Politics
Richard M. Valelly
9780195373851

American Political History
Donald Critchlow
9780199340057

American Political Parties and Elections
L. Sandy Maisel
9780195301229

The American Presidency
Charles O. Jones
9780195307016

Anarchism
Colin Ward
9780192804778

Borders
Alexander C. Diener &
Joshua Hagen
9780199731503

The British Constitution
Martin Loughlin
9780199697694

British Politics
Tony Wright
9780199661107

Capitalism
James Fulcher
9780192802187

Citizenship
Richard Bellamy
9780192802538

Communism
Leslie Holmes
9780199551545

Democracy
Bernard Crick
9780192802507

Diplomacy
Joseph M. Siracusa
9780199588503

Engels
Terrell Carver
9780192804662

The European Union
John Pinder & Simon
Underwood
9780199681693

Fascism
Kevin Passmore
9780199685363

Fundamentalism
Malise Ruthven
9780199212705

Geopolitics
Klaus Dodds
9780199676781

Globalization
Manfred B. Steger
9780199662661

Governance
Mark Bevir
9780199606412

International Migration
Khalid Koser
9780199298013

International Relations
Paul Wilkinson
9780192801579

International Security
Christopher S. Browning
9780199668533

Machiavelli
Quentin Skinner
9780192854070

Mao
Delia Davin
9780199588664

Marx
Peter Singer
9780192854056

Modern War
Richard English
9780199607891

Nationalism
Steven Grosby
9780192840981

Nelson Mandela
Elleke Boehmer
9780192803016

Neoliberalism
Manfred B. Steger
& Ravi K. Roy
9780199560516

Nuclear Power
Maxwell Irvine
9780199584970

Nuclear Weapons
Joseph M. Siracusa
9780199229543

The Palestinian-Israeli Conflict
Martin Bunton
9780199603930

Politics
Kenneth Minogue
9780192853882

Political Philosophy
David Miller
9780192803955

Postcolonialism
Robert J. C. Young
9780192801821

Progressivism
Walter Nugent
9780195311068

The Reagan Revolution
Gil Troy
9780195317107

Revolutions
Jack A. Goldstone
9780199858507

Socialism
Michael Newman
9780192804310

Terrorism
Charles Townshend
9780199603947

Tocqueville
Harvey Mansfield
9780195175394

The United Nations
Jussi M. Hanhimäki
9780195304374

The U.S. Congress
Donald A. Ritchie
9780195338317

Utopianism
Lyman Tower Sargent
9780199573400

Religion

Wonga-bashing won't save the Church of England

By Linda Woodhead

We are living through a very significant historical change: the collapse of the historic churches which have shaped British society and culture. The Church of England, by law established, is no exception. A survey I carried out with YouGov for the Westminster Faith Debates (June 2013) shows that in Great Britain as a whole only 11 per cent of young people in their 20s now call themselves Church of England or Anglican, compared to nearer half of over-70s. The challenge facing the Archbishop of Canterbury, Justin Welby, is to address this decline. But the initial indications suggest he may be heading in the wrong direction.

Consider the Archbishop's criticisms of Wonga and other payday loan providers. Most commentators were positive. Welby braved the revelation that the Church had a small investment in Wonga, took advantage of the media coverage, and managed to highlight an important issue. This is remarkable given that he didn't have any serious initiative to announce, for the Church doesn't have the wherewithal to set up the credit unions of which he spoke so favourably. Here, it seems, is a churchman with something to say, the ability to say it in a comprehensible fashion, and the courage to stand up for social justice. So what's the problem?

Providing care for the poorest in society was, historically, part of the Church's business. In the mid-20th century it happily joined forces with the state to nationalize this work. When the Thatcher government started to challenge the welfare consensus, the Church of England was quick to leap to the defence of the poor. Its 1985 report 'Faith in the City' greatly irritated Mrs Thatcher, just as Mrs Thatcher's 'Sermon on the Mound' greatly irritated the clergy.

I was near the heart of all this, straight out of university to my first job teaching in an Anglican theological college (seminary). In the wake of 'Faith in the City' it had been decreed that the students should be bundled off to 'urban priority areas' to 'get alongside the poor', and win their clerical spurs. Despite good intentions, I found the whole thing patronising and economically naive. Quite a lot of 'the poor' didn't seem to want to be got alongside. There was also a very obvious set of gender biases; the ideas were still of male clergy supporting working-class men. And the underpinning thinking was long on wealth distribution, short on wealth creation.

Fast forward to the last archbishop, Rowan Williams, a self-confessed 'beardy leftie'. Under his benevolent rule, the Church's focus on the poor and social justice remained remarkably similar to that of the 1980s, despite the fact that the category of 'the poor' had by this time become highly problematic. So when Rowan William's successor immediately turned his attention to 'the poorest in society', I heard the same old record going round.

The stuck-ness is concerning. What's worse is that this set of priorities is now strikingly out of step with the views of a majority of Anglicans, not to mention a majority of the British people. My YouGov poll finds that, even after correcting for age, most Anglicans fall on the 'free market' (in favour of individual enterprise) rather than the 'social welfare' (in favour of welfare and state interventions) side of the political values scale. Indeed, Anglicans are more tilted in that direction than the general population of the UK, even though the latter is also tilted towards 'free market' values. For example, just under half of all Anglicans, churchgoing or not, think that Mrs Thatcher did more good for Britain than did Tony Blair, compared with 38 per cent of the general population (16 per cent of Anglicans think Tony Blair did more good, compared with 18 per cent of the general population). And nearly 70 per cent of Anglicans believe that the welfare system has created a culture of dependency, which is almost ten percentage points higher than the general population.

But the real killer for the Church of England is that most people, including most Anglicans, are also out of step with official teaching on other issues of justice and fairness—most notably, the Church's policies with regards to women and gay people. To give him his due, the current archbishop has spoken strongly in favour of women bishops. But one of his earliest contributions to public life, even before Wonga, was to speak out strongly in the House of Lords against the legislation to allow gay marriage. Although he claimed that a majority of Anglicans are strongly opposed to this change, our poll shows that, on the contrary, Anglicans are now in favour of the proposed legislation by a small margin—as is the country as a whole, including, most overwhelmingly, younger people. My survey asked under-25s with negative views about the Church why they held those views. Not surprisingly, the most common answer was: 'The Church of England is too prejudiced—it discriminates against women and gay people.'

The problem which Justin Welby has to face is that you can't claim to be pro justice for some— 'the poor' —but not others—women and gay people. And since personal morality is the Church's core business, in a way welfare provision is not, those who still know their Bible may find a verse from Matthew springing to mind: 'Why beholdest thou the mote that is in thy brother's eye, but considerest not the beam that is in thine own eye?'

■ Linda Woodhead is the author of *Christianity: A Very Short Introduction*. 978-0-19-968774-9

Plato's mistake

By Norman Solomon

It started innocently enough at a lunch-time event with some friends at the Randolph Hotel in the centre of Oxford. 'The trouble with Islam . . . ' began some self-opinioned pundit, and I knew where he was going. Simple. Islam lends itself to fanaticism, and that is why Muslims perpetrate so much violence in the name of religion.

The pundit saw himself as Christian, and therefore a man of peace, so I had my cue. Look out of the window. Over there in the fork of the road you see the Martyr's Memorial. In 1555 the Wars of Religion were in full spate, Catholics were burning Protestants at the stake, Protestants were no less fanatical when their turn came, and things got even worse with the Civil War. So why are Muslims any worse?

'But that was 500 years ago. We've come a long way since then! And what about you, and all those atrocities in the Old Testament?' That stung me. Ignoramus—didn't he know that Judaism has moved a long way from the days of the ancient Hebrews?

'That was 2,500 years ago!' I retorted, and we moved on to a less contentious topic.

Being Jewish, I am of course impartial as between Christianity and Islam, both of which shout for peace but have bloody histories, with violence committed in the name of God by Christian against Christian, Muslim against Muslim, one against the other or either against some other unfortunate victim, such as the Jews.

But can I really wash my hands of all this? Not a Jewish problem, at least not for thousands of years? Well now, think again. The Bible is still a part of my history and I have to take some view on the fact that it often encourages violence in the name of God. We are about to celebrate the Jewish festival of Chanukah, so do I take sides with the 'valiant Maccabees' who—in God's name—carried on a guerrilla war against the Seleucids and eventually, with much bloodshed and mutual slaughter, gained control of Judea? (OK, the story is not in the Hebrew scriptures, and the events are more recent by a couple of centuries, but so what?) By modern standards the Maccabean warriors were violent religious fanatics. Judas Maccabeus is not the sort of man I would be comfortable to invite to tea; I would be pretty guarded in my answers if he asked me any awkward questions, and probably looking over my back to see if I was being watched by MI5, or the Seleucid equivalent. One person's religious fanatic is another person's freedom fighter; hardly an excuse, more like a choice between the devil and the deep blue sea.

The dilemma is ancient. Ambivalence towards past violence comes out in the way the rabbis told the story of Chanukah. There is a vague reference to some 'victory over the Greeks', but the kernel of the story is about a miracle that happened with a jar of oil when, following the victory, they rededicated the Jerusalem Temple. The idolatrous 'Greeks' had contaminated all the oil, but one jar was found with the high priest's seal still on it, and that miraculously lasted for eight days until pure oil could again be sourced. Nowhere else—in the copious contemporary or near-contemporary accounts of the military campaigns and of atrocities perpetrated by the 'other side'—is such a story mentioned. No. The rabbis retold the story their way, using it not to incite violence but to instil faith in God's saving grace. Which has at least dissociated them from the violence of the situation, even if from time to time others have revived the older stories and set up the Maccabees as models for emulation.

So why head this blog 'Plato's mistake'? Don't blame the Greeks! Because my Islamophobic friend and others like him, who generalize about Muslims, or Christians, or Jews, or whatever other group they happen to target, have fallen prey to just the error made by the great philosopher. It was Plato who dreamed up the notion of perfect forms (ideas) to which we can only aspire, and even though his own disciple Aristotle spotted the confusion, the error of essentialism took root and people still like to believe that there is some entity out there which is the 'true' Christianity, Islam, or Judaism, just as Plato taught there was a true 'good' whose existence was superior to anything on earth.

But there really is no such thing. 'Islam', 'Christianity', 'Judaism' are abstractions, not real things. What actually exists are Muslims, Christians, Jews—and of course, Hindus, Buddhist, Sikhs, and so on. Real individual people in relationship with others who share a common name. There are violent Muslims; it does not follow that 'Islam is violent', or that they are not 'really' Muslims. Conversely, I would not be right to claim, 'Judaism is peaceful'. All I can say is that this, that, or the other Jew is a peaceful person. All of us can tell our stories in many different ways. Some are violent, some peaceful.

Nor is the secular world different. Nationalism, socialism, and other secular creeds are all as variable as the individuals who take them on. Crimes have been committed in the name of each and every philosophy, and good has been done in the name of most of them too. It is not the creed that should shoulder the blame, but we ourselves.

■ Norman Solomon is the author of *Judaism: A Very Short Introduction*. 978-0-19-968735-0

Doubting Thomas: a patron saint for scientists?

By Thomas Dixon

The story of Doubting Thomas is a wonderful philosophical parable about seeing and believing, but what exactly is the intended moral? And what light does it shed on the relationship between science and religion?

The standard view portrays Doubting Thomas as a scientific hero demanding evidence and refusing to succumb to blind faith. Richard Dawkins has popularized this version since the publication of *The Selfish Gene* in 1976. Richard Dawkins tweeted, 'If there's evidence, it isn't faith. Doubting Thomas, patron saint of scientists, wanted evidence. Other disciples praised for not doing so.'

But this is not an entirely convincing interpretation either of the Bible or of the nature of scientific knowledge.

In John's gospel, the other disciples tell Thomas: 'We have seen the Lord.' Thomas is not convinced: 'Unless I see in his hands the print of the nails, and place my finger in the mark of the nails, and place my hand in his side, I will not believe.' A week later Jesus appears to all the disciples, and addresses Thomas: 'Put your finger here, and see my hands; and put out your hand and place it in my side; do not be faithless, but believing.' Thomas now believes, and Jesus comments: 'Blessed are those who have not seen and yet believe.'

Now, remember that according to Dawkins the story is told so that we should admire not Thomas, but the other disciples, 'whose faith was so strong that they did not need evidence'. What is wrong with that? Well, first of all, the other disciples believed in the resurrection not through blind faith, but because they saw the risen Jesus with their own eyes.

Dawkins is right that we are not supposed to admire Thomas's refusal to believe, but he is wrong about the reason. Thomas's behaviour really is a little irrational. What better basis for belief could he have had than the testimony of his most trusted friends? We all have to rely on testimony rather than first-hand experience for the vast majority of our knowledge.

Thomas's sin was the refusal to believe reliable testimony. The English natural philosopher and theologian John Wilkins wrote about the Doubting Thomas story in the 17th century. Jesus's saying, 'Blessed are those who have not seen and yet believe' signified, for Wilkins, that it was 'a more excellent, commendable and blessed thing for a man to yield his assent, upon such evidence as is in itself sufficient, without insisting upon more.' The testimony of the other disciples should have been in itself sufficient for Thomas; and yet he insisted upon more.

Communal observation and testimony are central to both religion and science. Caravaggio's *The Incredulity of St Thomas* (*c*.1601–2) depicts a collective act of witnessing. Should we, perhaps, even think of Thomas's finger here as a rudimentary scientific instrument? Is he making a digital measurement? Are the other disciples there to corroborate his observations? Rembrandt's slightly later painting of an anatomy lesson (1632) can be seen as a transposition of this model to a scientific setting. In both cases, the body of an executed criminal is being probed—in the case of Rembrandt's image, with forceps rather than just a finger—in front of a group of witnesses, and with the aim of producing knowledge.

The key point here is that these images depict acts of communal knowledge-production. Scientific knowledge, like religious belief, is produced by collaborative acts of observation which, in turn, rely on the observations, testimony, and inferences of others.

Richard Dawkins suggests that Doubting Thomas should be the patron saint of scientists. In fact he is patron saint of the blind, which is perhaps more fitting. If Thomas does stand for the view that the true basis of knowledge is unaided individual sense perception, then his is indeed an unscientific world and a world of blindness—a world where, in a phrase of Galileo, 'one wanders in vain through a dark labyrinth'. Galileo admired those who believed in the sun-centred system before the advent of the telescope: 'They have by sheer force of intellect done such violence to their own senses as to prefer what reason told them over that which sense experience plainly showed them to be the case.' Blessed, you might say, are those who have not seen and yet believe.

Returning to Caravaggio's painting, we see Thomas, his hand being taken by Christ and placed in the wound in his side. Thomas's eyes are dark, glazed, blank; he is gazing straight ahead, not at the wound. This is indeed a depiction of a blind man—a man being led by the hand towards something he cannot see. Caravaggio seems to say that the man who seeks to base all his knowledge on individual sense experience will see nothing. In both religion and science, the most important beliefs rest on a kind of seeing that cannot be done by an individual alone, that cannot be done with unaided human eyes, and that cannot be done without belief in an unseen realm.

■ Thomas Dixon is the author of *Science and Religion: A Very Short Introduction*. 978-0-19-929551-7

Is spirituality a passing trend?

By Philip Sheldrake

'Spirituality' is a word that defines our era. The fascination with spirituality is a striking aspect of our contemporary times and stands in stark contrast to the decline in traditional religious belonging in the West. Although the word 'spirituality' has Christian origins it has now moved well beyond these—indeed beyond religion itself.

What exactly is spirituality? Unfortunately it's not easy to offer a simple definition because the word is now widely used in contexts ranging from the major religions to the social sciences, psychology, the arts, and the professional worlds of, for example, healthcare, education, social work, and business studies. Spirituality takes on the shape and priorities of these different contexts.

However, in broad terms 'spirituality' stands for lifestyles and practices that embody a vision of how the human spirit can achieve its full potential. In other words, spirituality embraces an aspirational approach to the meaning and conduct of life—we are driven by goals beyond purely material success or physical satisfaction. Nowadays, spirituality is not the preserve of spiritual elites, for example in monasteries, but is presumed to be native to everyone. It is individually tailored, democratic, and eclectic, and offers an alternative source of inner-directed, personal authority in response to a decline of trust in conventional social or religious leaderships.

If we explore the wide range of current books on spirituality or browse the Web we will regularly find that spirituality involves a search for 'meaning'—the purpose of life. It also concerns what is 'holistic'—that is, an integrating factor, 'life seen as a whole'. Spirituality is also understood to be engaged with a quest for 'the sacred' —whether God, the numinous, the boundless mysteries of the universe, or our own human depths. The word is also regularly linked to 'thriving' —what it means to thrive and how we are enabled to thrive. Contemporary approaches also relate spirituality to a self-reflective existence in place of an unexamined life.

How is spirituality to be supported? The great wisdom traditions suggest the adoption of certain spiritual practices, and it is this aspect of spirituality that attracts many contemporary people. Forms of meditation, physical posture or movement such as yoga, disciplines of frugality and abstinence (for example from alcohol or meat), or visits to sacred sites and pilgrimage (for example, the popular practice of walking the *camino* to Santiago de Compostela) are among the most common. The point is that spiritual practices are not merely productive in a narrow sense, but are disciplined and creative. A commitment to the regularity of a spiritual discipline like meditation gives shape to what may otherwise be a fragmented life. Many people also experience their creative activities in art, music, writing, and so on as spiritual practices. Classic practices are all directed at spiritual development. Thus, meditation may cultivate stillness or attentiveness but the great religious traditions such as Buddhism or Christianity also relate such practices to personal transformation—whether in terms of personal ethics or increased social responsibility. Over time meditation may facilitate a growing freedom from destructive energies that inhibit healthy relationships. Such a growth in inner freedom makes us more available and effective as compassionate presences in the world.

It follows from this that, as the great traditions emphasize, spirituality is actually concerned with cultivating a 'spiritual life' rather than simply with undertaking practices isolated from commitment. It offers a 'value-added' factor to personal and professional lives. So, for example, in a variety of social contexts spirituality is believed to add two vital things. First, it saves us from being purely results-orientated. Thus, in health care it offers more than a medicalized, cure-focused model, and in education it suggests that a holistic approach to intellectual, moral, and social development is as vital as acquiring employable skills. Second, spirituality expands ethical behaviour by moving it beyond right or wrong actions to a question of identity—we are to be ethical people rather than simply to 'do' ethical things. Character formation and the cultivation of virtue then become central concerns.

Finally, is spirituality simply a passing trend? Current evidence suggests a growing diversity of new forms of spirituality as well as creative reinventions of the great traditions. The language of spirituality continues to expand into ever more professional and social worlds—for example urban planning and architecture, the corporate world, sport, and law. Most strikingly there are recent signs of its emergence in two contexts that have been especially open to public criticism—commerce and politics. Equally, the Internet is increasingly used to expand access to spiritual wisdom. So, on current evidence, spirituality appears to be less of a fad than an instinctive desire to find a deeper level of values to live by. As such, it seems likely not only to survive but to develop further into many new forms.

■ Philip Sheldrake is the author of *Spirituality: A Very Short Introduction*. 978-0-19-958875-6

Religion

Protestantism
Mark A. Noll
9780199560974

Puritanism
Francis J. Bremer
9780195334555

The Quakers
Pink Dandelion
9780199206797

Rastafari
Ennis B. Edmonds
9780199584529

Religion in America
Timothy Beal
9780195321074

Science and Religion
Thomas Dixon
9780199295517

Sikhism
Eleanor Nesbitt
9780192806017

Spirituality
Philip Sheldrake
9780199588756

Theology
David Ford
9780199679973

Tibetan Buddhism
Matthew T. Kapstein
9780199735129

Science

The value of networks

By Michele Catanzaro and Guido Caldarelli

Thanks to a single Facebook post in 2010, an extra 340,000 people went to vote in the 2010 USA Congress elections. This striking discovery, made by political scientist James Fowler and colleagues, reveals the extent to which social networks can influence the basic workings of democracy. Of course, Facebook is just one of the many networks in which people today have embedded themselves. Every day, a typical person might meet friends and colleagues, log in to email and twitter accounts, send text messages, and answer phone calls. There's more: when this typical person takes a plane, makes purchases, or transfers money, it implicates her in further networks. In an IT intensive society, all these actions leave tracks. This poses huge privacy protection questions, but it also provides an unprecedented opportunity to study people and networks quantitatively.

Centuries have passed since mathematician Leonard Euler showed for the first time that thinking in terms of networks can be extremely revealing: he solved the Königsberg bridge problem (can the seven bridges of the city of Königsberg all be traversed in a single trip without doubling back?) by applying logic in this way. Decades have passed since sociologists and psychologists started to draw maps of human relations. But the science of networks has still much to tell, and the current data deluge is giving it a second youth. So how has thinking in terms of 'networks' helped us in recent years?

1. The financial crisis

In a paper published in August 2012, physicist Stefano Battiston and his colleagues defined the DebtRank, a powerful tool to evaluate which banks would generate the worst consequences if defaulting. This measure is inspired by PageRank, the algorithm that allows Google to discover the most relevant pages on the web. Battiston's measure takes into account the network of stock ownership among banks, to identify those that are 'too central to fail' (in contrast with the classical 'too big to fail' paradigm). Such refined measures would be impossible without a networked approach to the large amount of financial data generated every day.

2. The 2009 swine flu pandemic

Old age plagues, like the Black Death, took years to spread. On the contrary, H1N1 jumped from one side of the planet to the opposite in a matter of weeks. The main difference between then and now? Modern infections have a powerful channel they can use to spread globally: the air flight network. Hence, the global map of airports' connections was used by physicist Alessandro Vespignani and his colleagues as the basis for modelling the spread of H1N1, and as a result they were able to forecast the peaks of the disease in different countries.

3. Offers of employment

In the 1970s, sociologist Marc Granovetter discovered the 'strength of weak ties': he concluded that it was easier to secure job offers through acquaintances than via close friends. Decades later, LinkedIn is one of the best applications of this discovery: people who have been contacted by headhunters or received offers through this social network know it well. Understanding how networks work can be very valuable to better handle relations, both online and offline.

4. Relationships: from Medici to Messi

'Cosimo de' Medici's leadership of 15th century Florence can be explained in part by his ability to make the most out of the network of relations between families in the city'; this paper in *The American Journal of Sociology* looked at how 'Medicean political control was produced by means of network disjunctures within the elite, which the Medici alone spanned'. Similarly, the differing performances of football player Lionel Messi when playing for Barcelona and Argentina can be partially understood when you consider the different pattern of relations between the other players in the two teams.

Criticism of network sciences should be taken seriously: risks can include unreliable data, carelessness with details, drastic simplifications in models, and fake trends. In general, scientists are, with reason, suspicious of holistic all-purpose 'theories of everything'. However, careful and intelligent application of network tools can continue to deliver a wealth of results in the future.

■ Michele Catanzaro and Guido Caldarelli are the authors of *Networks: A Very Short Introduction*. 978-0-19-958807-7

Animal evolution: a new view of an old tree

By Peter Holland

The metaphor of the 'evolutionary tree' is powerful. Closely related species, such as octopus and squid, can be pictured as twigs sitting near each other on a small branch, and in turn connected to larger and larger branches, each representing more distant evolutionary relationships. Every animal species, past and present, is a twig somewhere on the vast tree of life. But what is the shape of this metaphorical tree? Can we find the correct place for all the twigs, or perhaps even just the largest branches? In short, who is related to whom? To solve this would be to reconstruct the history of animal life on our planet.

Solving the puzzle is not simple. Even with just a hundred species, there are more possible trees than there are protons in the universe. And of course there are millions of animal species alive today, so the number of possible evolutionary trees is simply unimaginable. Yet remarkable progress has been made.

In 1857, Charles Darwin wrote to his friend Thomas Henry Huxley: 'The time will come, I believe, though I shall not live to see it, when we shall have fairly true genealogical trees of each great kingdom of nature.' Darwin did not live to see it. Through most of the 20th century, biologists argued fervently about the tree of animal life, with every expert having different opinions. For example, many felt that 'segmented worms', such as earthworms and leeches, must be close relatives of other segmented animals, such as insects and spiders. Perhaps simple-looking animals, such as flatworms and parasitic flukes, were on a branch emerging near the base of the animal tree of life. These were commonly held views, and are still found in many textbooks. They are, however, wrong.

In the 1990s, a new source of data emerged that has changed our view of animal evolution theory. There is a set of genes used by all animal cells and these genes accumulate mutations to their DNA sequences over time. The more closely related two species are, the more similar their DNA sequences. With new technologies it is possible to find the DNA sequence of hundreds of genes, from hundreds of species, and to amass vast data sets for comparison between species. In the light of this new information, many of the old arguments have melted away. And the DNA sequences give a remarkably consistent picture. It seems we can now describe the 'fairly true genealogical tree' of animal evolution, stretching back over half a billion years. We can deduce that soon after the origin of the first animals, most likely simple balls of cells, several major evolutionary branches separated. One branch led to sponges, one to comb jellies, one to a little-known group called placozoans, one to jellyfish and sea anemones, and one to the first 'bilaterians'. You and I are bilaterians, as are worms, snails, insects, and millions more: these are the animals with front and back, top and bottom, and left and right. The bilaterian part of the animal kingdom then split into three huge branches: the Lophotrochozoa (including snails, segmented worms, and many more), the Ecdysozoa (including insects, spiders, nematodes, and more), and the Deuterostomia (for example, starfish, sea urchins, and vertebrates). The vertebrates branched and branched again; giving ever smaller groups of closely related species, until eventually we found our own place in the great tree of life. Nestled among the apes, monkeys, and other primates, we sit on a mammalian branch along with, perhaps surprisingly, the rats, mice, and rabbits.

Why does knowing the tree of life matter? There are practical applications, because knowing which animals are closely related helps if we wish to extrapolate findings between species, for medical research, for instance. But there is a wider, more fundamental reason. Having the tree of life provides the essential framework for understanding biology. We can now compare anatomy, physiology, behaviour, ecology, and development between animal species in a more meaningful way than ever before. We can see how characters changed along each branch of the tree of life. In short, we can now start to build a picture of the pattern and process of animal evolution.

■ Peter Holland is the author of *The Animal Kingdom: A Very Short Introduction*. 978-0-19-959321-7

Astrobiology: pouring cold asteroid water on Aristotle

By David C. Catling

Over 2,300 years ago, in his book *De Caelo* (On the Heavens), Aristotle asked if other Earth-like worlds existed and then he dismissed the idea. But now, remarkably, the question is on the verge of being answered scientifically. NASA's Kepler space telescope, launched in 2009, has collected data on the statistical occurrence of small planets that orbit stars at a distance where it's the right temperature for liquid water and therefore conceivably for life. The endeavour of identifying potentially habitable planets is part of the convergence of astronomy, biology, and geology into astrobiology—the study of the origin and evolution of life on our own planet and the possible variety of life elsewhere.

In astrobiology, the need to assimilate different disciplines is illustrated by the factors that allow Earth-like planets to form. Someone familiar with astrophysics and geology can deduce that rocky planets are an expected consequence of the physics of starlight. Meanwhile, a scientist who knows planetary science and geochemistry will conclude that you drink asteroid water.

Consider starlight first. Hydrogen, helium, and a little lithium were made in the Big Bang, but all the other chemical elements are products of nuclear reactions inside stars. In the reactions, elements that are made up of whole numbers of fused helium atoms are favoured, including oxygen, magnesium, silicon, and iron. Rocky planets form from the dispersed remnants of old stars, and the four aforementioned elements dominate the minerals inside the Earth. So even before the Kepler telescope started finding exoplanets (planets around other stars), physics told us that Earth-like worlds should be out there. The nature of starlight preordains a cosmos teeming with rocky planets.

What about asteroid water? All the Earth's life-giving water had to come from somewhere. Rocky planets amalgamated out of a disk of material when the Solar System formed. Computer simulations show that icy asteroids that were scattered out of a region between Mars and Jupiter were responsible for bringing most of the water to the growing Earth. Furthermore, studies of water inside meteorites support the theory.

Of course, water is only one ingredient for life as we know it, so what else was needed? Signs of extinct life in ancient terrestrial rocks provide clues. Life originated on Earth at least 3.5 to 3.8 billion years ago. Then, afterwards, an alien landscape devoid of animals and large plants persisted for the next three billion years—in part because of the lack of abundant oxygen. In fact, genetics suggest that the common ancestor of all life today was a microbe that lived in conditions of 80–100°C and negligible oxygen. Today, the study of microbes in similar environments below the Earth's surface or in warm, fractured seafloor provides hints about early life.

Evolutionary obstacles may be the reason why it took a long time for single-celled life to evolve into animals and large plants. One tricky step was evolving the right type of cell. Of the three basic types on Earth, only eukaryote cells form large multicellular organisms, unlike the microbial cells of bacteria or archaea. A second hurdle was that the atmosphere had to become oxygen-rich to enable large organisms to exist and breathe. Astrobiologists study whether such steps were difficult or easy to provide insight into the possible prevalence of complex, Earth-like life elsewhere.

Unlike the demands of complex life, biologists have found microbes (extremophiles) that are adapted to environmental extremes such as temperature, acidity, pressure, and salinity. As a result, it's not unreasonable that extremophiles might live below the surface of Mars or in salty, high-pressure oceans deep inside the icy moons in the outer Solar System.

In fact, the possibility of life existing (or having existed) elsewhere in our own Solar System is far from settled. Mars gets the most press but many other bodies are candidates. Objects with possible subsurface seas and potential life include Ceres (the largest asteroid); Europa, Ganymede, and Callisto (moons of Jupiter); Titan, Enceladus, and Rhea (moons of Saturn); Titania and Oberon (moons of Uranus); Triton (Neptune's largest moon); and finally Pluto and similar icy dwarf planets beyond Pluto. Life may also have originated and gone extinct on ancient Venus before its surface evolved to today's hellish 460°C and an air pressure of 93 atmospheres pressure. Only future exploration can tell.

One certainty is that new discoveries of exoplanets promise a busy future for astrobiology. It's just a matter of time before we know about the atmospheres and surfaces of Earth-like exoplanets. Many peculiar worlds will also be found: dead planets with pure carbon-dioxide atmospheres, worlds covered entirely with glinting oceans, and young planets so close to their parent star that they're shedding atmospheres of steam into space. But on benign worlds, the possibility of life will be of intense interest. Welcome to astrobiology and trying to understand life here and elsewhere!

■ David C. Catling is the author of *Astrobiology: A Very Short Introduction*. 978-0-19-958645-5

The sustainability of civil engineering

By David Muir Wood

The definition of civil engineering is a historical curiosity. Originally so called to distinguish it from military engineering, it was particularly concerned (in the 18th century, for example) with the provision of infrastructure for transport, hence the French emphasis on *ponts et chaussées* in their organization of education and professional activity. But there is really no difference in the nature of the engineering performed by civil engineers and that performed by military engineers; a bridge or an airfield is a bridge or an airfield, whether it is provided for the general benefit of mankind or to enable an army to advance. Perhaps the speed of construction and the intended lifetime will be different—the latter often linked to the former. Charles Coulomb, who is remembered today by schoolchildren for his work on electrostatics (which makes him an electrical engineer), was employed by the army designing and constructing fortifications in Martinique (which makes him a military engineer), an activity which led to a nice piece of analysis which is familiar to all students of civil engineering today.

As a catch-all term, civil engineering in the early 19th century covered the broadest range of engineering activities but, for whatever reason, in the United Kingdom various splinter groups formed—mechanical engineers, electrical engineers, municipal engineers, aeronautical engineers, naval architects—and the engineering profession is littered with 'Institutions' for each of these professional groups which would originally have fallen under the aegis of the Institution of Civil Engineers.

The Institution of Civil Engineers was formed, we gather, in a coffee shop in Fleet Street (London) in 1818 by a group of engineers whose names are known but not familiar—it was only with the engagement of Thomas Telford as their first president that they gained some recognition, culminating in the award of a Royal Charter in 1828. Here for the first time an attempt was made by Thomas Tredgold to define civil engineering in words that have a wonderful 19th century beauty and resonance. The purpose of the newly fledged Institution was:

The general advancement of mechanical science, and more particularly for promoting the . . . acquisition of that species of knowledge which constitutes the profession of a civil engineer; being the art of directing the great sources of power in nature for the use and convenience of man, as the means of production and of traffic in states, both for external and internal trade, as applied in the construction of roads, bridges, aqueducts, canals, river navigation, and docks, for internal intercourse and exchange; and in the construction of ports, harbours, moles, breakwaters, and light-houses, and in the art of navigation by artificial power, for the purposes of commerce; and in the construction and adaptation of machinery, and in the drainage of cities and towns.

Many of those examples have been lost to other institutions but the phrase 'the art of directing the great sources of power in nature for the use and convenience of man' has remained. How would we describe civil engineering today? Can we continue to subscribe to this wonderful phrase of Thomas Tredgold's? Prince

Charles, in a lecture to the Institution of Civil Engineers, calls with typical gallo-principian passion for civil engineers committed to sustainability to turn Tredgold's phrase around and seek to be 'directed by nature', 'to understand and to work in harmony with nature's underlying patterns of behaviour.'

The problem with words is that you never know where they have been—or as Humpty-Dumpty said, 'When I use a word it means just what I choose it to mean—neither more nor less.' The nuances associated with Tredgold's words in 1828 are somewhat lost in dictionary definitions in 2013. It is the absence of any timescale that leaves the phrase open to attack. If we interpret 'man' as representing the human race, which implicitly includes our children and our children's children, then 'the use and convenience of man' contains a future positive intention of sustainability with regard to the sources of power in nature which goes beyond the negative possibility of present exploitation.

Is it a lack of linguistic confidence which might make us reluctant to displace a well-loved 19th century phrase in favour of a 21st century revisionist version? Or is it a recognition that, as with the *Book of Common Prayer*, there is something special about the original words and language? If we pause and seek to interpret them in our own time we will understand a deeper meaning relevant for us and for the future. If we insist on apparent instant sound-bite clarity we will be certain that we have understood without hearing and without thinking.

Prince Charles is right in urging civil engineers to concern themselves more vigorously with sustainability. But I do not think that we need to discard Thomas Tredgold as we do so.

■ David Muir Wood is the author of *Civil Engineering: A Very Short Introduction*. 978-0-19-957863-4

Science

Anaesthesia
Aidan O'Donnell
9780199584543

The Animal Kingdom
Peter Holland
9780199593217

The Antarctic
Klaus Dodds
9780199697687

Anxiety
Daniel Freeman & Jason
Freeman
9780199567157

Astrobiology
David C. Catling
9780199586455

Autism
Uta Frith
9780199207565

Bacteria
Sebastian Amyes
9780199578764

Borders
Alexander C. Diener &
Joshua Hagen
9780199731503

The Brain
Michael O'Shea
9780192853929

Cancer
Nick James
9780199560233

The Cell
Terence Allen &
Graham Cowling
9780199578757

Chaos
Leonard Smith
9780192853783

Child Psychology
Usha Goswami
9780199646593

Civil Engineering
David Muir Wood
9780199578634

Climate
Mark Maslin
9780199641130

Climate Change
Mark Maslin
9780198719045

Complexity
John H. Holland
9780199662548

The Computer
Darrel Ince
9780199586592

Consciousness
Susan Blackmore
9780192805850

Coral Reefs
Charles Sheppard
9780199682775

Cosmology
Peter Coles
9780192854162

Cryptography
Fred Piper & Sean Murphy
9780192803153

Darwin
Jonathan Howard
9780192854544

Deserts
Nick Middleton
9780199564309

Developmental Biology
Lewis Wolpert
9780199601196

Dinosaurs
David Norman
9780192804198

Dreaming
J. Allan Hobson
9780192802156

Drugs
Leslie Iversen
9780192854315

The Earth
Martin Redfern
9780192803078

The Elements
Philip Ball
9780192840998

Engineering
David Blockley
9780199578696

Epidemiology
Rodolfo Saracci
9780199543335

Evolution
Brian & Deborah
Charlesworth
9780192802514

The Eye
Michael F. Land
9780199680306

Food
John Krebs
9780199661084

Forensic Psychology
David Canter
9780199550203

Forensic Science
Jim Fraser
9780199558056

Fossils
Keith Thomson
9780192805041

Fractals
Kenneth Falconer
9780199675982

Freud
Anthony Storr
9780192854551

Galaxies
John Gribbin
9780199234349

Galileo
Stillman Drake
9780192854568

Game Theory
Ken Binmore
9780199218462

Genes
Jonathan Slack
9780199676507

Genius
Andrew Robinson
9780199594405

Geography
John A. Matthews & David T. Herbert
9780199211289

Global Catastrophes
Bill McGuire
9780198715931

The History of Astronomy
Michael Hoskin
9780192803061

The History of Life
Michael J. Benton
9780199226320

The History of Mathematics
Jacqueline Stedall
9780199599684

HIV/AIDS
Alan Whiteside
9780192806925

Hormones
Martin Luck
9780199672875

Human Evolution
Bernard Wood
9780192803603

The Ice Age
Jamie Woodward
9780199580699

Intelligence
Ian J. Deary
9780192893215

International Migration
Khalid Koser
9780199298013

Jung
Anthony Stevens
9780192854582

Landscapes and Geomorphology
Andrew Goudie & Heather Viles
9780199565573

The Laws of Thermodynamics
Peter Atkins
9780199572199

Madness
Andrew Scull
9780199608034

Magnetism
Stephen J. Blundell
9780199601202

Marine Biology
Philip V. Mladenov
9780199695058

Materials
Christopher Hall
9780199672677

Mathematics
Timothy Gowers
9780192853615

Medical Ethics
Tony Hope
9780192802828

Medical Law
Charles Foster
9780199660445

Memory
Jonathan K. Foster
9780192806758

Michael Faraday
Frank A. J. L. James
9780199574315

Microbiology
Nicholas P. Money
9780199681686

Minerals
David Vaughan
9780199682843

Molecules
Philip Ball
9780192854308

Networks
Guido Caldarelli & Michele Catanzaro
9780199588077

Newton
Rob Iliffe
9780199298037

Nothing
Frank Close
9780199225866

Numbers
Peter M. Higgins
9780199584055

Nuclear Power
Maxwell Irvine
9780199584970

Nutrition
David Bender
9780199681921

Particle Physics
Frank Close
9780199804341

The Periodic Table
Eric R. Scerri
9780199582495

Physical Chemistry
Peter Atkins
9780199689095

The Plague
Paul Slack
9780199589548

Planets
David A. Rothery
9780199573509

Plants
Timothy Walker
9780199584062

Probability
John Haigh
9780199588480

Psychiatry
Tom Burns
9780192807274

Psychology
Gillian Butler & Freda
McManus
9780199670420

Quantum Theory
John Polkinghorne
9780192802521

Radioactivity
Claudio Tuniz
9780199692422

Relativity
Russell Stannard
9780199236220

Rivers
Nick Middleton
9780199588671

Robotics
Alan Winfield
9780199695980

Schizophrenia
Chris Frith & Eve C.
Johnstone
9780192802217

Sexuality
Veronique Mottier
9780199298020

Sleep
Steven W. Lockley &
Russell G. Foster
9780199587858

Stars
Andrew King
9780199602926

Statistics
David J. Hand
9780199233564

Stem Cells
Jonathan Slack
9780199603381

Structural Engineering
David Blockley
9780199671939

Superconductivity
Stephen J. Blundell
9780199540907

Symmetry
Ian Stewart
9780199651986

Teeth
Peter S. Ungar
9780199670598

Viruses
Dorothy H. Crawford
9780199574858

Social Science

The demise of the toff

By William Doyle

Born to tenants of a country squire in Yorkshire, I knew about, what my grandmother called, 'toffs' at an early age. The squire was a toff. He owned the village and broad acres for miles around. He lived in a grand and beautiful Jacobean mansion. He had served in the Guards, collected pictures, and bred racehorses which the queen made a special journey to see. But he only enjoyed all this because his elder brother had died young, and, to help pay inheritance taxes, he sold land and opened his house to the public. And, without children of his own, he left the house and estate to distant relatives. He was the last of his line, and when he died, he was buried in the church where I was baptised, among his ancestors.

As a child I scarcely realized that the squire and his lifestyle were already relics of a fast-disappearing pattern of society. But when I grew up to be a historian, I found myself drawn to the 18th century, a time when the power and ostentation of such men was at its height throughout Europe. And in coming to specialize in the French Revolution, I had a ringside seat at the first occasion on which their claims to superiority came under open attack. The French revolutionaries saw their main enemies as aristocrats, by which they meant people claiming nobility, and anybody who accepted their pretensions. They attempted to abolish nobility, banned the use of titles, liveried servants, and the display of coats of arms, and revoked the special laws by which nobles had passed on their property down the generations. Many nobles reacted then to attacks on them by claiming that nobody could abolish a quality transmitted in their blood from ancestors who had earned it by deeds of valour. They were right that what they believed about themselves could not be abolished, and aristocracies survived the revolutionary onslaught. But in reality the vast majority of their members had never been descendants of long lines of noble ancestors, and most of the ancestors they did have had bought their nobility from the king. Fraudulent lineages were big business. Nobility, in fact, not simply in France but throughout Europe, was largely a set of myths designed to bolster and perpetuate the power structures of pre-industrial society.

It is important that we work to deconstruct these myths. The myths begin with the very word 'aristocracy', which strictly means 'government by the best people'. This of course begs the question of who the 'best' are. It is clear that throughout history they have mostly defined themselves, and that this definition has been determined by the rich, the powerful, and their clients. Until less than two centuries ago, that meant big landowners. The economic importance of agriculture was overwhelming, but those who dominated it always sought to decorate their power with display and distinctive lifestyles which emphasized cultural as well as economic superiority. They dressed differently, lived lavishly, rode rather than walked, scorned trade, and claimed special privileges as governors and defenders of the whole community. Men who made money other than in agriculture flocked as soon as they could afford it to join this power elite and hide their low origins. Aristocracies were seldom as exclusive as they hoped to appear. They needed new blood and new money to keep themselves going. Nobility was normally transmitted in the male line, but very few families can produce male heirs for more than a few successive generations. Broken lines of inheritance were much more normal. Marrying new money, however disdainfully, also regularly sustained the wealth essential to behaving like aristocrats.

Before the 18th century, nobody dreamed that things could be any other way. Aristocrats gave the tone to the rest of society, and many remnants of their cultural dominance remain with us, as any visitor to a stately home, or events such as horse trials, can see.

But once the French Revolution had shown aristocratic power to be vulnerable, it could no longer be taken for granted. 19th century industrialization and globalization then sapped the wealth of European agrarian elites and produced richer rivals, while the advent of democracy undermined their political power, in the very parliaments which were one of their most enduring legacies to later times. 20th century wars and social upheavals completed the shipwreck. Our collective memory is littered with aristocratic debris, and we instinctively use the term 'aristocratic' to describe anything superior or exclusive. But hereditary distinctions are no longer created, even in a country which still has a House of Lords. In time the last toffs will wither away, like the vanished forelock-tugging peasants over whom they lorded it for so long.

- William Doyle is the author of *Aristocracy: A Very Short Introduction*. 978-0-19-920678-0

Zeroing in on zero-hours work

By Stephen Fineman

The growth of zero-hours work contracts has grabbed the headlines recently. The contracts offer no guaranteed work hours and can swing between feast (over-work) and famine (literally nil hours). Employees are expected to be available as and when needed. If they refuse (which in principle they can) they risk being labelled as unreliable and overlooked the next time round.

No fixed hours means no fixed pay, and traditional benefits, such as holiday entitlements and sickness pay, can be minimal or non-existent. Zero-hours contracts have been a mainstay of the low-paid service industry (McDonald's has admitted to hiring all but a tiny proportion of its staff on that basis), and are common to social care, hotels, retail outlets, and even the UK's House of Commons and the hallowed Buckingham Palace.

The status of zero-hours sharply divides commentators—political and academic—broadly along left-wing/right-wing lines. Three perspectives are discernible:

1. Zero-hours are exploitative. They place undue power in the hands of the employer to do almost what they like with employees, providing them with little security or work predictability. It's turning back the clock on workers' rights.

2. Zero-hours are a manifestation of the 21st century patterns of work flexibility. They suit many people's lifestyles and are a lot better than being unemployed.

3. Concern about zero-hours is a distraction. They are a symptom of an economy adjusting to a recession and to little or no growth. Fix the economy and zero-hours will wither on the vine.

These contentions contain a degree of truth and a degree of fallacy. There are employers who take advantage of a large pool of unemployed; the work-desperate are at their disposal. Zero-hours contracts help an employer slim their overheads and extract, in Marxian terms, more surplus value from a large reserve of labour. Anecdotally, we know this can be oppressive to workers. They are unsure about what they will earn in a week, but they still have regular bills to pay (banks regard them as not credit worthy). They cannot risk absence for illness or to care for others in case it is used against them. Some feel treated like they are worthless.

Zero-hours endanger the hard-won rights of organized labour, so it is not surprising that unions are unnerved at the prospect. It is offensive. But zero-hours without the 'contract' word attached to it has long been the fate of low-skilled and migrant labour at the margins of Western capitalism, and far less marginal in parts of the world where the jobless gather each morning on street corners, by shipyards, and in front of factory gates in the hope that today they will be chosen for work.

The difficulty for Western societies is when zero-hours looks as if they are going mainstream, and here the evidence suggests that it is increasing but is proportionately small. However, small numbers do not blunt the moral case against major employers who use zero-hours as vehicles of convenience to increase already substantial profits on the backs of a vulnerable workforce. The situation seems different for small- and medium-sized enterprises that, without zero-hours, or some variant on them, would probably go bust. I am thinking here of the small workshop, the restaurant, bar, and garden centre, plumbers, builders, or seaside accommodation businesses, where seasonal and weekly fluctuations in business make planning very difficult.

Flexibility has become the mantra of the postmodern workplace and is often positively coupled with zero-hours. But flexible for whom? For instance, zero-hours are concentrated in the social care sector, but they undermine the continuity and familiarity that clients crave, and that care workers consider vital. The unpredictably of zero-hours—sporadic, irregular work—is challenging for families dependent on a single income or for single parents trying to juggle child care and work. As one zero-hourer explained, 'A job is better than no job, but not to know if you are working when you wake up is much sadder.' On the other hand, there are workers who are untroubled by zero-hours. They fit comfortably with their lifestyles, such as students dovetailing paid work with their studies, and retirees adding extra income and activity to their later years.

It is a comforting but naive assertion that zero-hours are no more than an unfortunate spike on the economic landscape, and that when markets pick up zero-hours will fade. The very existence of zero-hours sows seeds of worker disaffection and distrust, and adds to consumer lack of confidence. Zero-hours contracts have become part of the recovery problem, not simply a symptom of it. And I suspect that now the zero-hours' genie is out of the bottle, it is not to be easily reinserted; it serves some business interests too well. Zero hour on zero-hours is some way off.

■ Stephen Fineman is the author of *Work: A Very Short Introduction*. 978-0-19-969936-0

Social Sciences

Antisemitism
Steven Beller
9780192892775

Aristocracy
William Doyle
9780199206780

Education
Gary Thomas
9780199643264

Feminism
Margaret Walters
9780192805102

Food
John Krebs
9780199661084

HIV/AIDS
Alan Whiteside
9780192806925

Information
Luciano Floridi
9780199551378

Languages
Stephen Anderson
9780199590599

Multiculturalism
Ali Rattansi
9780199546039

Racism
Ali Rattansi
9780192805904

Sexuality
Veronique Mottier
9780199298020

Social and Cultural Anthropology
John Monaghan
& Peter Just
9780192853462

Sociology
Steve Bruce
9780192853806

Sport
Mike Cronin
9780199688340

Utopianism
Lyman Tower Sargent
9780199573400

Work
Stephen Fineman
9780199699360

Index of titles